THE ALEXANDER SHAKESPEARE

General Editor
R.B. Kennedy

Additional notes and e...
Mike Gould

AS YOU LIKE IT

William Shakespeare

COLLINS
CLASSICS

Harper Press
An imprint of HarperCollins*Publishers*
77–85 Fulham Palace Road
Hammersmith
London W6 8JB

This Harper Press paperback edition published 2011

A catalogue record for this book is available from the British Library

ISBN-13: 978-0-00-790239-2

Printed and bound in Great Britain by Clays Ltd, St Ives plc

Find out more about HarperCollins and the environment at
www.harpercollins.co.uk/green

Life & Times section © Gerard Cheshire
Introduction by Philip Hobsbaum
Shakespeare: Words and Phrases adapted from
Collins English Dictionary
Typesetting in Kalix by Palimpsest Book Production Limited,
Falkirk, Stirlingshire

10 9 8 7 6 5 4 3 2 1

Prefatory Note

This Shakespeare play uses the full Alexander text. By keeping in mind the fact that the language has changed considerably in four hundred years, as have customs, jokes, and stage conventions, the editors have aimed at helping the modern reader – whether English is their mother tongue or not – to grasp the full significance of the play. The Notes, intended primarily for examination candidates, are presented in a simple, direct style. The needs of those unfamiliar with British culture have been specially considered.

Since quiet study of the printed word is unlikely to bring fully to life plays that were written directly for the public theatre, attention has been drawn to dramatic effects which are important in performance. The editors see Shakespeare's plays as living works of art which can be enjoyed today on stage, film and television in many parts of the world.

CONTENTS

An Elizabethan playhouse. Note the apron stage protruding into the auditorium, the space below it, the inner room at the rear of the stage, the gallery above the inner stage, the canopy over the main stage, and the absence of a roof over the audience.

The Theatre in Shakespeare's Day

On the face of it, the conditions in the Elizabethan theatre were not such as to encourage great writers. The public playhouse itself was not very different from an ordinary inn-yard; it was open to the weather; among the spectators were often louts, pickpockets and prostitutes; some of the actors played up to the rowdy elements in the audience by inserting their own jokes into the authors' lines, while others spoke their words loudly but unfeelingly; the presentation was often rough and noisy, with fireworks to represent storms and battles, and a table and a few chairs to represent a tavern; there were no actresses, so boys took the parts of women, even such subtle and mature ones as Cleopatra and Lady Macbeth; there was rarely any scenery at all in the modern sense. In fact, a quick inspection of the English theatre in the reign of Elizabeth I by a time-traveller from the twentieth century might well produce only one positive reaction: the costumes were often elaborate and beautiful.

Shakespeare himself makes frequent comments in his plays about the limitations of the playhouse and the actors of his time, often apologizing for them. At the beginning of *Henry V* the Prologue refers to the stage as 'this unworthy scaffold' and to the theatre building (the Globe, probably) as 'this wooden O', and emphasizes the urgent need for imagination in making up for all the deficiencies of presentation. In introducing Act IV the Chorus goes so far as to say:

> . . . we shall much disgrace
> With four or five most vile and ragged foils,
> Right ill-dispos'd in brawl ridiculous,
> The name of Agincourt, (lines 49–52)

In *A Midsummer Night's Dream* (Act V, Scene i) he seems to dismiss actors with the words:

The best in this kind are but shadows.

Yet Elizabeth's theatre, with all its faults, stimulated dramatists to a variety of achievement that has never been equalled and, in Shakespeare, produced one of the greatest writers in history. In spite of all his grumbles he seems to have been fascinated by the challenge that it presented him with. It is necessary to re-examine his theatre carefully in order to understand how he was able to achieve so much with the materials he chose to use. What sort of place was the Elizabethan playhouse in reality? What sort of people were these criticized actors? And what sort of audiences gave them their living?

The Development of the Theatre up to Shakespeare's Time

For centuries in England noblemen had employed groups of skilled people to entertain them when required. Under Tudor rule, as England became more secure and united, actors such as these were given more freedom, and they often performed in public, while still acknowledging their 'overlords' (in the 1570s, for example, when Shakespeare was still a schoolboy at Stratford, one famous company was called 'Lord Leicester's Men'). London was rapidly becoming larger and more important in the second half of the sixteenth century, and many of the companies of actors took the opportunities offered to establish themselves at inns on the main roads leading to the City (for example, the Boar's Head in Whitechapel and the Tabard in South-wark) or in the City itself. These groups of actors would come to an agreement with the inn-keeper which would give them the use of the yard for their performances after people had eaten and drunk well in the middle of the day. Before long, some inns were taken over completely by companies of players and thus became the first public theatres. In 1574 the officials of the City of London issued an order which shows clearly that these theatres were both popular and also offensive to some respectable people, because the order complains about 'the inordinate haunting of great multitudes of people, specially youth, to plays interludes and shows; namely occasion of frays and quarrels, evil practices of incontinency in great inns . . .' There is evidence that, on public holidays, the theatres on the banks of the Thames were crowded with noisy apprentices and tradesmen, but it would be wrong to think that audiences were always undiscriminating and loudmouthed. In spite of the disapproval of Puritans and the more staid members of society, by the 1590s, when Shakespeare's plays were beginning to be performed, audiences consisted of a good cross-section of English society, nobility as well as workers, intellectuals as well as simple people out for a laugh; also (and in this respect English theatres were unique in Europe), it was quite normal for respectable women to attend plays. So Shakespeare had to write plays which would appeal to people of widely different kinds. He had to provide 'something for everyone' but at the same time to take care to unify the material so that it would not seem to fall into separate pieces as they watched it. A speech like that of the drunken porter in *Macbeth* could provide the 'groundlings' with a belly-laugh, but also held a deeper significance for those who could appreciate it. The audience he wrote for was one of a number of apparent drawbacks which Shakespeare was able to turn to his and our advantage.

Shakespeare's Actors

Nor were all the actors of the time mere 'rogues, vagabonds and sturdy beggars' as some were described in a Statute of 1572. It is true that many of them had a hard life and earned very little money, but leading actors could become partners in the ownership of the theatres in which they acted: Shakespeare was a shareholder in the Globe and the Blackfriars theatres when he was an actor as well as a playwright. In any case, the attacks made on Elizabethan actors were usually directed at their morals and not at their acting ability; it is clear that many of them must have been good at their trade if they were able to interpret complex works like the great tragedies in such a way as to attract enthusiastic audiences. Undoubtedly some of the boys took the women's parts with skill and confidence, since a man called Coryate, visiting Venice in 1611, expressed surprise that women could act as well as they: 'I saw women act, a thing that I never saw before . . . and they performed it with as good a grace, action, gesture . . . as ever I saw any masculine actor.' The quality of most of the actors who first presented Shakespeare's plays is probably accurately summed up by Fynes Moryson, who wrote, '. . . as there be, in my opinion, more plays in London than in all the parts of the world I have seen, so do these players or comedians excel all other in the world.'

The Structure of the Public Theatre

Although the 'purpose-built' theatres were based on the inn-yards which had been used for play-acting, most of them were circular. The walls contained galleries on three storeys from which the wealthier patrons watched, they must have been something like the 'boxes' in a modern theatre, except that they held much larger numbers – as many as 1500. The 'groundlings' stood on the floor of the building, facing a raised stage which projected from the 'stage-wall', the main features of which were:

1 a small room opening on to the back of the main stage and on the same level as it (rear stage),
2 a gallery above this inner stage (upper stage),
3 canopy projecting from above the gallery over the main stage, to protect the actors from the weather (the 700 or 800 members of the audience who occupied the yard, or 'pit' as we call it today, had the sky above them).

In addition to these features there were dressing-rooms behind the stage and a space underneath it from which entrances could be made through trap-doors. All the acting areas – main stage, rear stage, upper stage and under stage – could be entered by actors directly from their dressing rooms, and all of them were used in productions of Shakespeare's plays. For example, the inner stage, an almost cavelike structure, would have been where Ferdinand and Miranda are 'discovered' playing chess in the last act of *The Tempest*, while the upper stage was certainly the balcony from which Romeo climbs down in Act III of *Romeo and Juliet*.

It can be seen that such a building, simple but adaptable, was not really unsuited to the presentation of plays like Shakespeare's. On the contrary, its simplicity guaranteed the minimum of distraction, while its shape and construction must have produced a sense of involvement on the part of the audience that modern producers would envy.

Other Resources of the Elizabethan Theatre

Although there were few attempts at scenery in the public theatre (painted backcloths were occasionally used in court performances), Shakespeare and his fellow playwrights were able to make use of a fair variety of 'properties', lists of such articles have survived: they include beds, tables, thrones, and also trees, walls, a gallows, a Trojan horse and a 'Mouth of Hell'; in a list of properties belonging to the manager, Philip Henslowe, the curious item 'two mossy banks' appears. Possibly one of them was used for the

> bank whereon the wild thyme blows,
> Where oxlips and the nodding violet grows

in *A Midsummer Night's Dream* (Act II, Scene i). Once again, imagination must have been required of the audience.

Costumes were the one aspect of stage production in which

trouble and expense were hardly ever spared to obtain a magnificent effect. Only occasionally did they attempt any historical accuracy (almost all Elizabethan productions were what we should call 'modern-dress' ones), but they were appropriate to the characters who wore them: kings were seen to be kings and beggars were similarly unmistakable. It is an odd fact that there was usually no attempt at illusion in the costuming: if a costume looked fine and rich it probably was. Indeed, some of the costumes were almost unbelievably expensive. Henslowe lent his company £19 to buy a cloak, and the Alleyn brothers, well-known actors, gave £20 for a 'black velvet cloak, with sleeves embroidered all with silver and gold, lined with black satin striped with gold'.

With the one exception of the costumes, the 'machinery' of the playhouse was economical and uncomplicated rather than crude and rough, as we can see from this second and more leisurely look at it. This meant that playwrights were stimulated to produce the imaginative effects that they wanted from the language that they used. In the case of a really great writer like Shakespeare, when he had learned his trade in the theatre as an actor, it seems that he received quite enough assistance of a mechanical and structural kind without having irksome restrictions and conventions imposed on him; it is interesting to try to guess what he would have done with the highly complex apparatus of a modern television studio. We can see when we look back to his time that he used his instrument, the Elizabethan theatre, to the full, but placed his ultimate reliance on the communication between his imagination and that of his audience through the medium of words. It is, above all, his rich and wonderful use of language that must have made play-going at that time a memorable experience for people of widely different kinds. Fortunately, the deep satisfaction of appreciating and enjoying Shakespeare's work can be ours also, if we are willing to overcome the language difficulty produced by the passing of time.

Shakespeare: A Timeline

Very little indeed is known about Shakespeare's private life; the facts included here are almost the only indisputable ones. The dates of Shakespeare's plays are those on which they were first produced.

1558 Queen Elizabeth crowned.

1561 Francis Bacon born.

1564 Christopher Marlowe born.

      William Shakespeare born, April 23rd, baptized April 26th.

1566

      Shakespeare's brother, Gilbert, born.

1567 Mary, Queen of Scots, deposed.
James VI (later James I of England) crowned King of Scotland.

1572 Ben Jonson born.
Lord Leicester's Company (of players) licensed; later called Lord Strange's, then the Lord Chamberlain's and finally (under James) the King's Men.

1573 John Donne born.

1574 The Common Council of London directs that all plays and playhouses in London must be licensed.

1576 James Burbage builds the first public playhouse, The Theatre, at Shoreditch, outside the walls of the City.

1577 Francis Drake begins his voyage round the world (completed 1580).
Holinshed's Chronicles of England, Scotland and Ireland published (which

Shakespeare later used
extensively).

1582		Shakespeare married to Anne Hathaway.
1583	The Queen's Company founded by royal warrant.	Shakespeare's daughter, Susanna, born.
1585		Shakespeare's twins, Hamnet and Judith, born.
1586	Sir Philip Sidney, the Elizabethan ideal 'Christian knight', poet, patron, soldier, killed at Zutphen in the Low Countries.	
1587	Mary, Queen of Scots, beheaded. Marlowe's *Tamburlaine (Part I)* first staged.	
1588	Defeat of the Spanish Armada. Marlowe's *Tamburlaine (Part II)* first staged.	
1589	Marlowe's *Jew of Malta* and Kyd's *Spanish Tragedy* (a 'revenge tragedy' and one of the most popular plays of Elizabethan times).	
1590	Spenser's *Faerie Queene* (Books I–III) published.	
1592	Marlowe's *Doctor Faustus* and *Edward II* first staged. Witchcraft trials in Scotland. Robert Greene, a rival playwright, refers to Shakespeare as 'an upstart crow' and 'the only Shake-scene in a country'.	*Titus Andronicus* *Henry VI, Parts I, II and III* *Richard III*
1593	London theatres closed by the plague. Christopher Marlowe killed in a Deptford tavern.	*Two Gentlemen of Verona* *Comedy of Errors* *The Taming of the Shrew* *Love's Labour's Lost*
1594	Shakespeare's company becomes The Lord Chamberlain's Men.	*Romeo and Juliet*

1595	Raleigh's first expedition to Guiana. Last expedition of Drake and Hawkins (both died).	*Richard II* *A Midsummer Night's Dream*
1596	Spenser's *Faerie Queene* (Books IV–VI) published. James Burbage buys rooms at Blackfriars and begins to convert them into a theatre.	*King John* *The Merchant of Venice* Shakespeare's son Hamnet dies. Shakespeare's father is granted a coat of arms.
1597	James Burbage dies, his son Richard, a famous actor, turns the Blackfriars Theatre into a private playhouse.	*Henry IV (Part I)* Shakespeare buys and redecorates New Place at Stratford.
1598	Death of Philip II of Spain	*Henry IV (Part II)* *Much Ado About Nothing*
1599	Death of Edmund Spenser. The Globe Theatre completed at Bankside by Richard and Cuthbert Burbage.	*Henry V* *Julius Caesar* *As You Like It*
1600	Fortune Theatre built at Cripplegate. East India Company founded for the extension of English trade and influence in the East. The Children of the Chapel begin to use the hall at Blackfriars.	*Merry Wives of Windsor* *Troilus and Cressida*
1601		*Hamlet*
1602	Sir Thomas Bodley's library opened at Oxford.	*Twelfth Night*
1603	Death of Queen Elizabeth. James I comes to the throne. Shakespeare's company becomes The King's Men. Raleigh tried, condemned and sent to the Tower	
1604	Treaty of peace with Spain	*Measure for Measure* *Othello* *All's Well that Ends Well*
1605	The Gunpowder Plot: an attempt by a group of Catholics to blow up the Houses of Parliament.	

1606	Guy Fawkes and other plotters executed.	*Macbeth* *King Lear*
1607	Virginia, in America, colonized. A great frost in England.	*Antony and Cleopatra* *Timon of Athens* *Coriolanus* Shakespeare's daughter, Susanna, married to Dr. John Hall.
1608	The company of the Children of the Chapel Royal (who had performed at Blackfriars for ten years) is disbanded. John Milton born. Notorious pirates executed in London.	Richard Burbage leases the Blackfriars Theatre to six of his fellow actors, including Shakespeare. *Pericles, Prince of Tyre*
1609		Shakespeare's Sonnets published.
1610	A great drought in England	*Cymbeline*
1611	Chapman completes his great translation of the *Iliad*, the story of Troy. Authorized Version of the Bible published.	*A Winter's Tale* *The Tempest*
1612	Webster's *The White Devil* first staged.	Shakespeare's brother, Gilbert, dies.
1613	Globe theatre burnt down during a performance of *Henry VIII* (the firing of small cannon set fire to the thatched roof). Webster's *Duchess of Malfi* first staged.	*Henry VIII* *Two Noble Kinsmen* Shakespeare buys a house at Blackfriars.
1614	Globe Theatre rebuilt in 'far finer manner than before'.	
1616	Ben Jonson publishes his plays in one volume. Raleigh released from the Tower in order to prepare an expedition to the gold mines of Guiana.	Shakespeare's daughter, Judith, marries Thomas Quiney. Death of Shakespeare on his birthday, April 23rd.
1618	Raleigh returns to England and is executed on the charge for which he was imprisoned in 1603.	
1623	Publication of the Folio edition of Shakespeare's plays	Death of Anne Shakespeare (née Hathaway).

Life & Times

William Shakespeare the Playwright

There exists a curious paradox when it comes to the life of William Shakespeare. He easily has more words written about him than any other famous English writer, yet we know the least about him. This inevitably means that most of what is written about him is either fabrication or speculation. The reason why so little is known about Shakespeare is that he wasn't a novelist or a historian or a man of letters. He was a playwright, and playwrights were considered fairly low on the social pecking order in Elizabethan society. Writing plays was about providing entertainment for the masses – the great unwashed. It was the equivalent to being a journalist for a tabloid newspaper.

In fact, we only know of Shakespeare's work because two of his friends had the foresight to collect his plays together following his death and have them printed. The only reason they did so was apparently because they rated his talent and thought it would be a shame if his words were lost.

Consequently his body of work has ever since been assessed and reassessed as the greatest contribution to English literature. That is despite the fact that we know that different printers took it upon themselves to heavily edit the material they worked from. We also know that Elizabethan plays were worked and reworked frequently, so that they evolved over time until they were honed to perfection, which means that many different hands played their part in the active writing process. It would therefore be fair to say that any play attributed to Shakespeare is unlikely to contain a great deal of original input. Even the plots were based on well known historical events, so it would be hard to know what fragments of any Shakespeare play came from that single mind.

One might draw a comparison with the Christian bible, which remains such a compelling read because it came from the collaboration of many contributors and translators over centuries, who each adjusted the stories until they could no longer be improved. As virtually nothing is known of Shakespeare's life and even less about his method of working, we shall never know the truth about his plays. They certainly contain some very elegant phrasing, clever plot devices and plenty of words never before seen in print, but as to whether Shakespeare invented them from a unique imagination or whether he simply took them from others around him is anyone's guess.

The best bet seems to be that Shakespeare probably took the lead role in devising the original drafts of the plays, but was open to collaboration from any source when it came to developing them into workable scripts for effective performances. He would have had to work closely with his fellow actors in rehearsals, thereby finding out where to edit, abridge, alter, reword and so on.

In turn, similar adjustments would have occurred in his absence, so that definitive versions of his plays never really existed. In effect Shakespeare was only responsible for providing the framework of plays, upon which others took liberties over time. This wasn't helped by the fact that the English language itself was not definitive at that time either. The consequence was that people took it upon themselves to spell words however they pleased or to completely change words and phrasing to suit their own preferences.

It is easy to see then, that Shakespeare's plays were always going to have lives of their own, mutating and distorting in detail like Chinese whispers. The culture of creative preservation was simply not established in Elizabethan England. Creative ownership of Shakespeare's plays was lost to him as soon as he released them into the consciousness of others. They saw nothing wrong with taking his ideas and running with them, because no one had ever suggested that one shouldn't, and Shakespeare probably regarded his work in the same way. His plays weren't sacrosanct works of art, they were templates for theatre folk to make their livings from, so they had every right to mould them into productions that drew in the crowds as effectively as possible. Shakespeare was like the helmsman of a sailing ship, steering the vessel but wholly reliant on the team work of his crew to arrive at the desired destination.

It seems that Shakespeare certainly had a natural gift, but the genius of his plays may be attributable to the collective efforts of Shakespeare and others. It is a rather satisfying notion to think that *his* plays might actually be the creative outpourings of the Elizabethan milieu in which Shakespeare immersed himself. That makes them important social documents as well as seminal works of the English language.

Money in Shakespeare's Day

It is extremely difficult, if not impossible, to relate the value of money in our time to its value in another age and to compare prices of commodities today and in the past. Many items *are* simply not comparable on grounds of quality or serviceability.

There was a bewildering variety of coins in use in Elizabethan England. As nearly all English and European coins were gold or silver, they had intrinsic value apart from their official value. This meant that foreign coins circulated freely in England and were officially recognized, for example the French crown (écu) worth about 30p (72 cents), and the Spanish ducat worth about 33p (79 cents). The following table shows some of the coins mentioned by Shakespeare and their relation to one another.

GOLD	British	American	SILVER	British	American
sovereign (heavy type)	£1.50	$3.60	shilling	10p	24c
sovereign (light type)	66p–£l	$1.58–$2.40	groat	1.5p	4c
angel					
royal	33p–50p	79c–$1.20			
noble	50p	$1.20			
crown	25p	60c			

A comparison of the following prices in Shakespeare's time with the prices of the same items today will give some idea of the change in the value of money.

ITEM	PRICE British	American	ITEM	PRICE British	American
beef, per lb.	0.5p	1c	cherries (lb.)	1p	2c
mutton, leg	7.5p	18c	7 oranges	1p	2c
rabbit	3.5p	9c	1 lemon	1p	2c
chicken	3p	8c	cream (quart)	2.5p	6c
potatoes (lb)	10p	24c	sugar (lb.)	£1	$2.40
carrots (bunch)	1p	2c	sack (wine) (gallon)	14p	34c
8 artichokes	4p	9c	tobacco (oz.)	25p	60c
1 cucumber	1p	2c	biscuits (lb.)	12.5p	30c

INTRODUCTION

As You Like It is a pastoral, in which no naturalistic business of life distracts the attention of the audience from the emotions deployed among the various characters. The central character is Rosalind, daughter of a Duke exiled to the Forest of Arden, in turn herself expelled from her father's former dominion. She is accompanied by her cousin, Celia, and by a singularly loutish clown.

Rosalind has disguised herself as a boy. In this guise, she good-humouredly interrogates various characters, finding out who they are and exposing their various absurdities. There is, for example, a shepherdess who scorns her faithful lover. She is shrewdly told by Rosalind, 'Down on your knees,/And thank heaven, fasting, for a good man's love'. Another character thus catechised is Jaques, a worldly-wise cynic, whose satire is reductive and therefore no match for Rosalind's wholesome comedy. Jaques declares 'Why, 'tis good to be sad and say nothing' to be met with Rosalind's retort, 'Why then, 'tis good to be a post'.

But the crucial dialogues are those with Orlando, a young man from a surbordinate fiefdom, expelled, like the Duke, by a wicked brother. In her disguise as a boy, Rosalind enters into a mock-courtship, as it must necessarily be. But mock or not, this is a way of testing Orlando out, finding out who he really is. Rosalind, in her 'holiday humour', demands 'What would you say to me now, an I were your very very Rosalind?' to which he replies, in his romantic innocence, 'I would kiss before I spoke'. This romantic attitude is instantly debunked, in a decidedly pithy prose: 'Nay, you were better speak first; and when you were gravelled for lack of matter, you might take occasion to kiss. Very good orators, when they are out, they will spit; and for lovers lacking – God warn us! – matter, the cleanliest shift is to kiss'. That is not romantic, not redolent of Arden, but very much down to earth and of this world. Rosalind is not against love, but she is definitely against nonsense; as, indeed, is the play itself.

It is an interesting irony that Shakespeare uses the form of the pastoral to put forward a highly unpastoral set of attitudes. The medium is mostly prose, though prose of a racy and cheerful kind, as instanced in Rosalind's various rejoinders. The point can best be made if we contrast the language of *As You Like It* with that of *Rosalynde* by Thomas Lodge, from which it was adapted: ''Tis good, forester, to love, but not to overlove, lest in loving her that likes not thee, thou fold thyself in an endless labyrinth'.

Rosalynde is just a tale for the tale's own sake. *As You Like It*, on the other hand, has a definite pattern, though the text as we have it seems not quite finished, so there are some loose ends and internal contradictions. In the main, however, the worthwhile characters are chivvied from sensibility into sense, while the less worthwhile characters fall victim to various tricks. For example, the egregious Jaques seeks out a guru, who will no doubt addle his brains still further, and the loutish clown, Touchstone, marries one of the very 'country copulatives' whom he has, up till now, scorned.

The whole ends with an epilogue, spoken by Rosalind in her woman's dress once more: 'I charge you, O women, for the love you bear to men, to like as much of this play as please you'. This goes along with the title, *As You Like It*. The argument may seem circular, but the import is clear: test out fancy by acquaintance, and ignore the dictates of fashion. The Forest of Arden is a good place for self-discovery, but, once the 'self' is discovered, the characters troop back to town.

LIST OF CHARACTERS

Duke	living in exile
Frederick	his brother, and usurper of his dominions
Amiens *Jaques* }	lords attending on the banished Duke
Le Beau	a courtier attending upon Frederick
Charles	wrestler to Frederick
Oliver *Jaques* *Orlando* }	sons of Sir Rowland de Boys
Adam, Dennis	servants to Oliver
Touchstone	the court jester
Sir Oliver Martext	a vicar
Corin, Silvius	shepherds
William	a country fellow, in love with Audrey
A person representing *Hymen*	
Rosalind	daughter to the banished Duke
Celia	daughter to Frederick
Phebe	a shepherdess
Audrey	a country wench
Lords, Pages, Foresters, and *Attendants*	

The scene: Oliver's house; Frederick's court; and the forest of Arden.

ACT ONE
Scene I

Orchard of Oliver's house.

[Enter ORLANDO *and* ADAM.*]*

Orlando

As I remember, Adam, it was upon this fashion bequeathed me by will but poor a thousand crowns, and, as thou say'st, charged my brother, on his blessing, to breed me well; and there begins my sadness. My brother Jaques he keeps at school, and report speaks goldenly of his profit. For my part, he keeps me rustically at home, or, to speak more properly, stays me here at home unkept; for call you that keeping for a gentleman of my birth that differs not from the stalling of an ox? His horses are bred better; for, besides that they are fair with their feeding, they are taught their manage, and to that end riders dearly hir'd; but I, his brother, gain nothing under him but growth; for the which his animals on his dunghills are as much bound to him as I. Besides this nothing that he so plentifully gives me, the something that nature gave me his countenance seems to take from me. He lets me feed with his hinds, bars me the place of a brother, and as much as in him lies, mines my gentility with my education. This is it, Adam, that grieves me; and the spirit of my father, which I think is within me, begins to mutiny against this servitude. I will no longer endure it, though yet I know no wise remedy how to avoid it. 5 10 15 20

[Enter OLIVER.*]*

Adam

Yonder comes my master, your brother.

Orlando

25   Go apart, Adam, and thou shalt hear how he will shake
     me up. *[ADAM retires.]*

Oliver

Now, sir! what make you here?

Orlando

Nothing; I am not taught to make any thing.

Oliver

What mar you then, sir?

Orlando

30   Marry, sir, I am helping you to mar that which God
     made, a poor unworthy brother of yours, with
     idleness.

Oliver

Marry, sir, be better employed, and be nought awhile.

Orlando

Shall I keep your hogs, and eat husks with them? What
35   prodigal portion have I spent that I should come to
     such penury?

Oliver

Know you where you are, sir?

Orlando

O, sir, very well; here in your orchard.

Oliver

Know you before whom, sir?

Orlando

40   Ay, better than him I am before knows me. I know
     you are my eldest brother; and, in the gentle condition
     of blood, you should so know me. The courtesy of
     nations allows you my better in that you are the first-
     born; but the same tradition takes not away my blood,
45   were there twenty brothers betwixt us. I have as much
     of my father in me as you, albeit I confess your coming
     before me is nearer to his reverence.

Oliver

What, boy! *[Strikes him.]*

Orlando

Come, come, elder brother, you are too young in this.

Oliver

    Wilt thou lay hands on me, villain?   50

Orlando

    I am no villain; I am the youngest son of Sir Rowland
de Boys. He was my father; and he is thrice a villain
that says such a father begot villains. Wert thou not
my brother, I would not take this hand from thy throat
till this other had pull'd out thy tongue for saying so. 55
Thou has rail'd on thyself.

Adam

    [Coming forward] Sweet masters, be patient; for your
father's remembrance, be at accord.

Oliver

    Let me go, I say.

Orlando

    I will not, till I please; you shall hear me. My father 60
charg'd you in his will to give me good education: you
have train'd me like a peasant, obscuring and hiding
from me all gentleman-like qualities. The spirit of my
father grows strong in me, and I will no longer endure
it; therefore allow me such exercises as may become a 65
gentleman, or give me the poor allottery my father left
me by testament; with that I will go buy my fortunes.

Oliver

    And what wilt thou do? Beg, when that is spent? Well,
sir, get you in. I will not long be troubled with you;
you shall have some part of your will. I pray you leave 70
me.

Orlando

    I will no further offend you than becomes me for my
good.

Oliver

    Get you with him, you old dog.

Adam

    Is 'old dog' my reward? Most true, I have lost my teeth 75
in your service. God be with my old master! He would
not have spoke such a word. *[Exeunt* ORLANDO *and*
ADAM.*]*

Oliver

Is it even so? Begin you to grow upon me? I will physic
your rankness, and yet give no thousand crowns
80   neither. Holla, Dennis!

[Enter DENNIS.]

Dennis

Calls your worship?

Oliver

Was not Charles, the Duke's wrestler, here to speak
with me?

Dennis

So please you, he is here at the door and importunes
85   access to you.

Oliver

Call him in. *[Exit DENNIS]* 'Twill be a good way; and
to-morrow the wrestling is.

[Enter CHARLES.]

Charles

Good morrow to your worship.

Oliver

Good Monsieur Charles! What's the new news at the
90   new court?

Charles

There's no news at the court, sir, but the old news;
that is, the old Duke is banished by his younger brother
the new Duke; and three or four loving lords have put
themselves into voluntary exile with him, whose lands
95   and revenues enrich the new Duke; therefore he gives
them good leave to wander.

Oliver

Can you tell if Rosalind, the Duke's daughter, be
banished with her father?

Charles

O, no; for the Duke's daughter, her cousin, so loves
100   her, being ever from their cradles bred together, that

she would have followed her exile, or have died to
stay behind her. She is at the court, and no less beloved
of her uncle than his own daughter; and never two
ladies loved as they do.

Oliver

Where will the old Duke live? 105

Charles

They say he is already in the Forest of Arden, and a
many merry men with him; and there they live like
the old Robin Hood of England. They say many young
gentlemen flock to him every day, and fleet the time
carelessly, as they did in the golden world. 110

Oliver

What, you wrestle to-morrow before the new Duke?

Charles

Marry, do I, sir; and I came to acquaint you with a
matter. I am given, sir, secretly to understand that your
younger brother, Orlando, hath a disposition to come
in disguis'd against me to try a fall. To-morrow, sir, I 115
wrestle for my credit; and he that escapes me without
some broken limb shall acquit him well. Your brother
is but young and tender; and, for your love, I would
be loath to foil him, as I must, for my own honour,
if he come in; therefore, out of my love to you, I came 120
hither to acquaint you withal, that either you might
stay him from his intendment, or brook such disgrace
well as he shall run into, in that it is a thing of his
own search and altogether against my will.

Oliver

Charles, I thank thee for thy love to me, which thou 125
shalt find I will most kindly requite. I had myself notice
of my brother's purpose herein, and have by underhand
means laboured to dissuade him from it; but he is
resolute. I'll tell thee, Charles, it is the stubbornest
young fellow of France; full of ambition, an envious 130
emulator of every man's good parts, a secret and
villainous contriver against me his natural brother.

Therefore use thy discretion: I had as lief thou didst break his neck as his finger. And thou wert best look
135   to't; for it thou dost him any slight disgrace, or if he do not mightily grace himself on thee, he will practise against thee by poison, entrap thee by some treacherous device, and never leave thee till he hath ta'en thy life by some indirect means or other; for, I assure thee,
140   and almost with tears I speak it, there is not one so young and so villainous this day living. I speak but brotherly of him; but should I anatomize him to thee as he is, I must blush and weep, and thou must look pale and wonder.

Charles
145   I am heartily glad I came hither to you. If he come to-morrow I'll give him his payment. If ever he go alone again, I'll never wrestle for prize more. And so, God keep your worship!

[Exit.]

Oliver

Farewell, good Charles. Now will I stir this gamester.
150   I hope I shall see an end of him; for my soul, yet I know not why, hates nothing more than he. Yet he's gentle; never school'd and yet learned; full of noble device; of all sorts enchantingly beloved; and, indeed, so much in the heart of the world, and especially of
155   my own people, who best know him, that I am altogether misprised. But it shall not be so long; this wrestler shall clear all. Nothing remains but that I kindle the boy thither, which now I'll go about. *[Exit.]*

Scene II

A lawn before the Duke's palace.

[Enter ROSALIND *and* CELIA.*]*

Celia

I pray thee, Rosalind, sweet my coz, be merry.

Rosalind

Dear Celia, I show more mirth than I am mistress of; and would you yet I were merrier? Unless you could teach me to forget a banished father, you must not learn me how to remember any extraordinary pleasure. 5

Celia

Herein I see thou lov'st me not with the full weight that I love thee. If my uncle, thy banished father, had banished thy uncle, the Duke my father, so thou hadst been still with me, I could have taught my love to take thy father for mine; so wouldst thou, if the truth of 10 thy love to me were so righteously temper'd as mine is to thee.

Rosalind

Well, I will forget the condition of my estate, to rejoice in yours.

Celia

You know my father hath no child but I, nor none is 15 like to have; and, truly, when he dies thou shalt be his heir; for what he hath taken away from thy father perforce, I will render thee again in affection. By mine honour, I will; and when I break that oath, let me turn monster; therefore, my sweet Rose, my dear Rose, be 20 merry.

Rosalind

From henceforth I will, coz, and devise sports. Let me see; what think you of falling in love?

Celia

Marry, I prithee, do, to make sport withal; but love no man in good earnest, nor no further in sport neither 25

than with safety of a pure blush thou mayst in honour
come off again.

Rosalind

What shall be our sport, then?

Celia

30   Let us sit and mock the good housewife Fortune from
her wheel, that her gifts may henceforth be bestowed
equally.

Rosalind

I would we' could do so; for her benefits are mightily
misplaced; and the bountiful blind woman doth most
mistake in her gifts to women.

Celia

35   'Tis true; for those that she makes fair she scarce makes
honest; and those that she makes honest she makes
very ill-favouredly.

Rosalind

Nay; now thou goest from Fortune's office to Nature's:
Fortune reigns in gifts of the world, not in the linea-
40   ments of Nature.

[Enter TOUCHSTONE.*]*

Celia

No; when Nature hath made a fair creature, may she
not by Fortune fall into the fire? Though Nature hath
given us wit to flout at Fortune, hath not Fortune sent
in this fool to cut off the argument?

Rosalind

45   Indeed, there is Fortune too hard for Nature, when
Fortune makes Nature's natural the cutter-off of
Nature's wit.

Celia

Peradventure this is not Fortune's work neither, but
Nature's, who perceiveth our natural wits too dull to
50   reason of such goddesses, and hath sent this natural
for our whetstone; for always the dullness of the fool
is the whetstone of the wits. How now, wit! Whither
wander you?

Touchstone

Mistress, you must come away to your father.

Celia

Were you made the messenger?   55

Touchstone

No, by mine honour; but I was bid to come for you.

Rosalind

Where learned you that oath, fool?

Touchstone

Of a certain knight that swore by his honour they were good pancakes, and swore by his honour the mustard was naught. Now I'll stand to it, the pancakes were 60 naught and the mustard was good, and yet was not the knight forsworn.

Celia

How prove you that, in the great heap of your knowledge?

Rosalind

Ay, marry, now unmuzzle your wisdom.   65

Touchstone

Stand you both forth now: stroke your chins, and swear by your beards that I am a knave.

Celia

By our beards, if we had them, thou art.

Touchstone

By my knavery, if I had it, then I were. But if you swear by that that is not, you are not forsworn; no 70 more was this knight, swearing by his honour, for he never had any; or if he had, he had sworn it away before ever he saw those pancakes or that mustard.

Celia

Prithee, who is't that thou mean'st?

Touchstone

One that old Frederick, your father, loves.   75

Celia

My father's love is enough to honour him. Enough, speak no more of him; you'll be whipt for taxation one of these days.

Touchstone

80 The more pity that fools may not speak wisely what
wise men do foolishly.

Celia

By my troth, thou sayest true; for since the little wit that
fools have was silenced, the little foolery that wise men
have makes a great show. Here comes Monsieur Le Beau.

[Enter LE BEAU.]

Rosalind

With his mouth full of news.

Celia

85 Which he will put on us as pigeons feed their young.

Rosalind

Then shall we be news-cramm'd.

Celia

All the better; we shall be the more marketable. Bon
jour, Monsieur Le Beau. What's the news?

Le Beau

Fair Princess, you have lost much good sport.

Celia

90 Sport! of what colour?

Le Beau

What colour, madam? How shall I answer you?

Rosalind

As wit and fortune will.

Touchstone

Or as the Destinies decrees.

Celia

Well said; that was laid on with a trowel.

Touchstone

95 Nay, if I keep not my rank –

Rosalind

Thou losest thy old smell.

Le Beau

You amaze me, ladies. I would have told you of good
wrestling, which you have lost the sight of.

Rosalind

Yet tell us the manner of the wrestling.

Le Beau

I will tell you the beginning, and, if it please your 100
ladyships, you may see the end; for the best is yet to
do; and here, where you are, they are coming to
perform it.

Celia

Well, the beginning that is dead and buried.

Le Beau

There comes an old man and his three sons – 105

Celia

I could match this beginning with an old tale.

Le Beau

Three proper young men, of excellent growth and
presence.

Rosalind

With bills on their necks: 'Be it known unto all men
by these presents' – 110

Le Beau

The eldest of the three wrestled with Charles, the
Duke's wrestler; which Charles in a moment threw
him, and broke three of his ribs, that there is little
hope of life in him. So he serv'd the second, and so
the third. Yonder they lie; the poor old man, their 115
father, making such pitiful dole over them that all the
beholders take his part with weeping.

Rosalind

Alas!

Touchstone

But what is the sport, monsieur, that the ladies have
lost? 120

Le Beau

Why, this that I speak of.

Touchstone

Thus men may grow wiser every day. It is the first time
that ever I heard breaking of ribs was sport for ladies.

Celia

Or I, I promise thee.

Rosalind

125   But is there any else longs to see this broken music in his sides? Is there yet another dotes upon rib-breaking? Shall we see this wrestling, cousin?

Le Beau

You must, if you stay here; for here is the place appointed for the wrestling, and they are ready to

130   perform it.

Celia

Yonder, sure, they are coming. Let us now stay and see it.

[Flourish. Enter DUKE FREDERICK, LORDS, ORLANDO, CHARLES, *and Attendants.]*

Duke Frederick

Come on; since the youth will not be entreated, his own peril on his forwardness.

Rosalind

135   Is yonder the man?

Le Beau

Even he, madam.

Celia

Alas, he is too young; yet he looks successfully.

Duke Frederick

How now, daughter and cousin! Are you crept hither to see the wrestling?

Rosalind

140   Ay, my liege; so please you give us leave.

Duke Frederick

You will take little delight in it, I can tell you, there is such odds in the man. In pity of the challenger's youth I would fain dissuade him, but he will not be entreated. Speak to him, ladies; see if you can move him.

Celia

145   Call him hither, good Monsieur Le Beau.

Duke Frederick
Do so; I'll not be by.

[DUKE FREDERICK goes apart.]

Le Beau
Monsieur the Challenger, the Princess calls for you.
Orlando
I attend them with all respect and duty.
Rosalind
Young man, have you challeng'd Charles the
wrestler?   150
Orlando
No, fair Princess; he is the general challenger. I come
but in, as others do, to try, with him the strength of
my youth.
Celia
Young gentleman, your spirits are too bold for your
years. You have seen cruel proof of this man's strength; 155
if you saw yourself with your eyes, or knew yourself
with your judgment, the fear of your adventure would
counsel you to a more equal enterprise. We pray you,
for your own sake, to embrace your own safety and
give over this attempt.   160
Rosalind
Do, young sir; your reputation shall not therefore be
misprised: we will make it our suit to the Duke that
the wrestling might not go forward.
Orlando
I beseech you, punish me not with your hard
thoughts, wherein I confess me much guilty to deny 170
so fair and excellent ladies any thing. But let your
fair eyes and gentle wishes go with me to my trial;
wherein if I be foil'd, there is but one sham'd that
was never gracious; if kill'd, but one dead that is
willing to be so. I shall do my friends no wrong, for 175
I have none to lament me; the world no injury, for
in it I have nothing; only in the world I fill up a

place, which may be better supplied when I have
made it empty.

Rosalind

180   The little strength that I have, I would it were with
you.

Celia

And mine to eke out hers.

Rosalind

Fare you well. Pray heaven I be deceiv'd in you!

Celia

Your heart's desires be with you!

Charles

180   Come, where is this young gallant that is so desirous
to lie with his mother earth?

Orlando

Ready, sir; but his will hath in it a more modest
working.

Duke Frederick

You shall try but one fall.

Charles

185   No, I warrant your Grace, you shall not entreat him
to a second, that have so mightily persuaded him from
a first.

Orlando

You mean to mock me after; you should not have
mock'd me before; but come your ways.

Rosalind

190   Now, Hercules be thy speed, young man!

Celia

I would I were invisible, to catch the strong fellow by
the leg. *[They wrestle.]*

Rosalind

O excellent young man!

Celia

If I had a thunderbolt in mine eye, I can tell who
195   should down.

[CHARLES is thrown. Shout.]

Duke Frederick
No more, no more.
Orlando
Yes, I beseech your Grace; I am not yet well breath d.
Duke Frederick
How dost thou, Charles?
Le Beau
He cannot speak, my lord.
Duke Frederick
Bear him away. What is thy name, young man?   200
Orlando
Orlando, my liege; the youngest son of Sir Rowland
de Boys.
Duke Frederick
I would thou hadst been son to some man else.
The world esteem'd thy father honourable,
But I did find him still mine enemy.   205
Thou shouldst have better pleas'd me with this deed,
Hadst thou descended from another house.
But fare thee well; thou art a gallant youth;
I would thou hadst told me of another father.

[Exeunt DUKE, TRAIN, and LE BEAU.]

Celia
Were I my father, coz, would I do this?   210
Orlando
I am more proud to be Sir Rowland's son,
His youngest son – and would not change that
    calling
To be adopted heir to Frederick.
Rosalind
My father lov'd Sir Rowland as his soul,
And all the world was of my father's mind;   215
Had I before known this young man his son,
I should have given him tears unto entreaties
Ere he should thus have ventur'd.

Celia

                              Gentle cousin,
Let us go thank him, and encourage him;
220   My father's rough and envious disposition
Sticks me at heart. Sir, you have well deserv'd;
If you do keep your promises in love
But justly as you have exceeded all promise,
Your mistress shall be happy.

Rosalind

                              Gentleman,

[Giving him a chain from her neck.]

225   Wear this for me; one out of suits with fortune,
That could give more, but that her hand lacks means.
Shall we go, coz?

Celia

                    Ay. Fare you well, fair gentleman.

Orlando

Can I not say 'I thank you'? My better parts
Are all thrown down; and that which here stands up
230   Is but a quintain, a mere lifeless block.

Rosalind

He calls us back. My pride fell with my fortunes;
I'll ask him what he would. Did you call, sir?
Sir, you have wrestled well, and overthrown
More than your enemies.

Celia

                         Will you go, coz?

Rosalind

235   Have with you. Fare you well.

[Exeunt ROSALIND *and* CELIA.*]*

Orlando

What passion hangs these weights upon my tongue?
I cannot speak to her, yet she urg'd conference.
O poor Orlando, thou art overthrown!
Or Charles or something weaker masters thee.

[Re-enter LE BEAU.]

Le Beau

    Good sir, I do in friendship counsel you   240
    To leave this place. Albeit you have deserv'd
    High commendation, true applause, and love,
    Yet such is now the Duke's condition
    That he misconstrues all that you have done.
    The Duke is humorous; what he is, indeed,   245
    More suits you to conceive than I to speak of.

Orlando

    I thank you, sir; and pray you tell me this:
    Which of the two was daughter of the Duke
    That here was at the wrestling?

Le Beau

    Neither his daughter, if we judge by manners;   250
    But yet, indeed, the smaller is his daughter;
    The other is daughter to the banish'd Duke,
    And here detain'd by her usurping uncle,
    To keep his daughter company; whose loves
    Are dearer than the natural bond of sisters.   255
    But I can tell you that of late this Duke
    Hath ta'en displeasure 'gainst his gentle niece,
    Grounded upon no other argument
    But that the people praise her for her virtues
    And pity her for her good father's sake;   260
    And, on my life, his malice 'gainst the lady
    Will suddenly break forth. Sir, fare you well.
    Hereafter, in a better world than this,
    I shall desire more love and knowledge of you.

Orlando

    I rest much bounden to you; fare you well.   265
      [Exit LE BEAU.]
    Thus must I from the smoke into the smother;
    From tyrant Duke unto a tyrant brother.
    But heavenly Rosalind!

               [Exit.]

Scene III

The Duke's palace.

[Enter CELIA *and* ROSALIND.*]*

Celia
Why, cousin! why, Rosalind! Cupid have mercy! Not
a word?

Rosalind
Not one to throw at a dog.

Celia
No, thy words are too precious to be cast away upon
5   curs; throw some of them at me; come, lame me with
reasons.

Rosalind
Then there were two cousins laid up, when the one
should be lam'd with reasons and the other mad
without any.

Celia
10   But is all this for your father?

Rosalind
No, some of it is for my child's father.
O, how full of briers is this working-day world!

Celia
They are but burs, cousin, thrown upon thee in holiday
foolery; if we walk not in the trodden paths, our very
15   petticoats will catch them.

Rosalind
I could shake them off my coat: these burs are in my
heart.

Celia
Hem them away

Rosalind
I would try, if I could cry 'hem' and have him.

Celia
20   Come, come, wrestle with thy affections.

Rosalind

O, they take the part of a better wrestler than myself.

Celia

O, a good wish upon you! You will try in time, in despite of a fall. But, turning these jests out of service, let us talk in good earnest. Is it possible, on such a sudden, you should fall into so strong a liking with 25
old Sir Rowland's youngest son?

Rosalind

The Duke my father lov'd his father dearly.

Celia

Doth it therefore ensue that you should love his son dearly? By this kind of chase I should hate him, for my father hated his father dearly; yet I hate not 30
Orlando.

Rosalind

No, faith, hate him not, for my sake.

Celia

Why should I not? Doth he not deserve well?

[Enter DUKE FREDERICK, *with* LORDS.*]*

Rosalind

Let me love him for that; and do you love him because
I do. Look, here comes the Duke. 35

Celia

With his eyes full of anger.

Duke Frederick

Mistress, dispatch you with your safest haste,
And get you from our court.

Rosalind

           Me, uncle?

Duke Frederick

                 You, cousin.
Within these ten days if that thou beest found
So near our public court as twenty miles, 40
Thou diest for it.

Rosalind

          I do beseech your Grace,

Let me the knowledge of my fault bear with me.
If with myself I hold intelligence,
Or have acquaintance with mine own desires;
45   If that I do not dream, or be not frantic –
As I do trust I am not – then, dear uncle,
Never so much as in a thought unborn
Did I offend your Highness.

Duke Frederick

                         Thus do all traitors;
If their purgation did consist in words,
50   They are as innocent as grace itself.
Let it suffice thee that I trust thee not.

Rosalind

Yet your mistrust cannot make me a traitor.
Tell me whereon the likelihood depends.

Duke Frederick

Thou art thy father's daughter; there's enough.

Rosalind

55   So was I when your Highness took his dukedom;
So was I when your Highness banish'd him.
Treason is not inherited, my lord;
Or, if we did derive it from our friends,
What's that to me? My father was no traitor.
60   Then, good my liege, mistake me not so much
To think my poverty is treacherous.

Celia

Dear sovereign, hear me speak.

Duke Frederick

Ay, Celia; we stay'd her for your sake,
Else had she with her father rang'd along.

Celia

65   I did not then entreat to have her stay;
It was your pleasure, and your own remorse;
I was too young that time to value her,
But now I know her. If she be a traitor,
Why so am I: we still have slept together,
70   Rose at an instant, learn'd, play'd, eat together,

And wheresoe'er we went, like Juno's swans,
Still we went coupled and inseparable.

Duke Frederick

She is too subtle for thee; and her smoothness,
Her very silence and her patience,
Speak to the people, and they pity her.   75
Thou art a fool. She robs thee of thy name;
And thou wilt show more bright and seem more
    virtuous
When she is gone. Then open not thy lips.
Firm and irrevocable is my doom
Which I have pass'd upon her; she is banish'd.   80

Celia

Pronounce that sentence, then, on me, my liege;
I cannot live out of her company.

Duke Frederick

You are a fool. You, niece, provide yourself.
If you outstay the time, upon mine honour,
And in the greatness of my word, you die.   85

[Exeunt DUKE and LORDS.]

Celia

O my poor Rosalind! Whither wilt thou go?
Wilt thou change fathers? I will give thee mine.
I charge thee be not thou more griev'd than I am.

Rosalind

I have more cause.

Celia

                    Thou hast not, cousin.
Prithee be cheerful. Know'st thou not the Duke   90
Hath banish'd me, his daughter?

Rosalind

                              That he hath not.

Celia

No, hath not? Rosalind lacks, then, the love
Which teacheth thee that thou and I am one.
Shall we be sund'red? Shall we part, sweet girl?

95   No; let my father seek another heir.
      Therefore devise with me how we may fly,
      Whither to go, and what to bear with us;
      And do not seek to take your charge upon you,
      To bear your griefs yourself, and leave me out;
100   For, by this heaven, now at our sorrows pale,
      Say what thou canst, I'll go along with thee.
  Rosalind
      Why, whither shall we go?
  Celia
      To seek my uncle in the Forest of Arden.
  Rosalind
      Alas, what danger will it be to us,
105   Maids as we are, to travel forth so far!
      Beauty provoketh thieves sooner than gold.
  Celia
      I'll put myself in poor and mean attire,
      And with a kind of umber smirch my face;
      The like do you; so shall we pass along,
      And never stir assailants.
  Rosalind
100   Were it not better,
      Because that I am more than common tall,
      That I did suit me all points like a man?
      A gallant curtle-axe upon my thigh,
      A boar spear in my hand; and – in my heart
115   Lie there what hidden woman's fear there will –
      We'll have a swashing and a martial outside,
      As many other mannish cowards have
      That do outface it with their semblances.
  Celia
      What shall I call thee when thou art a man?
  Rosalind
120   I'll have no worse a name than Jove's own page,
      And therefore look you call me Ganymede.
      But what will you be call'd?

Celia

> Something that hath a reference to my state:
> No longer Celia, but Aliena.

Rosalind

> But, cousin, what if we assay'd to steal   125
> The clownish fool out of your father's court?
> Would he not be a comfort to our travel?

Celia

> He'll go along o'er the wide world with me;
> Leave me alone to woo him. Let's away,
> And get our jewels and our wealth together;   130
> Devise the fittest time and safest way
> To hide us from pursuit that will be made
> After my flight. Now go we in content
> To liberty, and not to banishment.

[Exeunt.]

ACT TWO

Scene I

The Forest of Arden.

[Enter DUKE SENIOR, AMIENS, and two or three LORDS, like foresters.]

Duke Senior

Now, my co-mates and brothers in exile,
Hath not old custom made this life more sweet
Than that of painted pomp? Are not these woods
More free from peril than the envious court?

5 Here feel we not the penalty of Adam,
The seasons' difference; as the icy fang
And churlish chiding of the winter's wind,
Which when it bites and blows upon my body,
Even till I shrink with cold, I smile and say

10 'This is no flattery; these are counsellors
That feelingly persuade me what I am'.
Sweet are the uses of adversity;
Which, like the toad, ugly and venomous,
Wears yet a precious jewel in his head;

15 And this our life, exempt from public haunt,
Finds tongues in trees, books in the running
        brooks,
Sermons in stones, and good in everything.
I would not change it.

Amiens

                        Happy is your Grace,
That can translate the stubbornness of fortune

20 Into so quiet and so sweet a style.

Duke Senior

Come, shall we go and kill us venison?
And yet it irks me the poor dappled fools,
Being native burghers of this desert city,

Should, in their own confines, with forked heads
Have their round haunches gor'd.
1 Lord

                   Indeed, my lord,   25
The melancholy Jaques grieves at that;
And, in that kind, swears you do more usurp
Than doth your brother that hath banish'd you.
To-day my Lord of Amiens and myself
Did steal behind him as he lay along   30
Under an oak whose antique root peeps out
Upon the brook that brawls along this wood!
To the which place a poor sequest'red stag,
That from the hunter's aim had ta'en a hurt,
Did come to languish; and, indeed, my lord,   35
The wretched animal heav'd forth such groans
That their discharge did stretch his leathern coat
Almost to bursting; and the big round tears
Cours'd one another down his innocent nose
In piteous chase; and thus the hairy fool,   40
Much marked of the melancholy Jaques,
Stood on th' extremest verge of the swift brook,
Augmenting it with tears.
Duke Senior

                But what said Jaques?
Did he not moralize this spectacle?
1 Lord

O, yes, into a thousand similes.   45
First, for his weeping into the needless stream:
'Poor deer,' quoth he 'thou mak'st a testament
As worldlings do, giving thy sum of more
To that which had too much'. Then, being there
    alone,
Left and abandoned of his velvet friends: 50
''Tis right;' quoth he 'thus misery doth part
The flux of company'. Anon, a careless heard,
Full of the pasture, jumps along by him
And never stays to greet him. 'Ay,' quoth Jaques

55 'Sweep on, you fat and greasy citizens;
    'Tis just the fashion. Wherefore do you look
    Upon that poor and broken bankrupt there?'
    Thus most invectively he pierceth through
    The body of the country, city, court,
60 Yea, and of this our life; swearing that we
    Are mere usurpers, tyrants, and what's worse,
    To fright the animals, and to kill them up
    In their assign'd and native dwelling-place.
Duke Senior
    And did you leave him in this contemplation?
2 Lord
65 We did, my lord, weeping and commenting
    Upon the sobbing deer.
Duke Senior
                           Show me the place;
    I love to cope him in these sullen fits,
    For then he's full of matter.
1 Lord
    I'll bring you to him straight. *[Exeunt.]*

Scene II

The Duke's palace.

[Enter DUKE FREDERICK, with LORDS.]

Duke Frederick
Can it be possible that no man saw them?
It cannot be; some villains of my court
Are of consent and sufferance in this.

1 Lord
I cannot hear of any that did see her.
The ladies, her attendants of her chamber,   5
Saw her abed, and in the morning early
They found the bed untreasur'd of their mistress.

2 Lord
My lord, the roynish clown, at whom so oft
Your Grace was wont to laugh, is also missing.
Hisperia, the Princess' gentlewoman,   10
Confesses that she secretly o'erheard
Your daughter and her cousin much commend
The parts and graces of the wrestler
That did but lately foil the sinewy Charles;
And she believes, wherever they are gone,   15
That youth is surely in their company.

Duke Frederick
Send to his brother; fetch that gallant hither.
If he be absent, bring his brother to me;
I'll make him find him. Do this suddenly;
And let not search and inquisition quail   20
To bring again these foolish runaways.

[Exeunt.]

Scene III

Before Oliver's house.

[Enter ORLANDO and ADAM, meeting.]

Orlando
    Who's there?
Adam
    What, my young master? O my gentle master!
    O my sweet master! O you memory
    Of old Sir Rowland! Why, what make you here?
5   Why are you virtuous? Why do people love you?
    And wherefore are you gentle, strong, and valiant?
    Why would you be so fond to overcome
    The bonny prizer of the humorous Duke?
    Your praise is come too swiftly home before you.
10   Know you not, master, to some kind of men
    Their graces serve them but as enemies?
    No more do yours. Your virtues, gentle master,
    Are sanctified and holy traitors to you.
    O, what a world is this, when what is comely
15   Envenoms him that bears it!
Orlando
    Why, what's the matter?
Adam
                         O unhappy youth!
    Come not within these doors; within this roof
    The enemy of all your graces lives.
    Your brother – no, no brother; yet the son –
20   Yet not the son; I will not call him son
    Of him I was about to call his father –
    Hath heard your praises; and this night he means
    To burn the lodging where you use to lie,
    And you within it. If he fail of that,
25   He will have other means to cut you off;
    I overheard him and his practices.
    This is no place; this house is but a butchery;

Abhor it, fear it, do not enter it.

Orlando

Why, whither, Adam, wouldst thou have me go?

Adam

No matter whither, so you come not here.   30

Orlando

What, wouldst thou have me go and beg my food,
Or with a base and boist'rous sword enforce
A thievish living on the common road?
This I must do, or know not what to do;
Yet this I will not do, do how I can.   35
I rather will subject me to the malice
Of a diverted blood and bloody brother.

Adam

But do not so. I have five hundred crowns,
The thrifty hire I sav'd under your father,
Which I did store to be my foster-nurse,   40
When service should in my old limbs lie lame,
And unregarded age in corners thrown.
Take that, and He that doth the ravens feed,
Yea, providently caters for the sparrow,
Be comfort to my age! Here is the gold;   45
All this I give you. Let me be your servant;
Though I look old, yet I am strong and lusty;
For in my youth I never did apply
Hot and rebellious liquors in my blood,
Nor did not with unbashful forehead woo   50
The means of weakness and debility;
Therefore my age is as a lusty winter,
Frosty, but kindly. Let me go with you;
I'll do the service of a younger man
In all your business and necessities.   55

Orlando

O good old man, how well in thee appears
The constant service of the antique world,
When service sweat for duty, not for meed!
Thou art not for the fashion of these times,

60   Where none will sweat but for promotion,
      And having that do choke their service up
      Even with the having; it is not so with thee.
      But, poor old man, thou prun'st a rotten tree
      That cannot so much as a blossom yield
65   In lieu of all thy pains and husbandry.
      But come thy ways, we'll go along together,
      And ere we have thy youthful wages spent
      We'll light upon some settled low content.

   Adam
      Master, go on; and I will follow thee
70   To the last gasp, with truth and loyalty.
      From seventeen years till now almost four-score
      Here lived I, but now live here no more.
      At seventeen years many their fortunes seek,
      But at fourscore it is too late a week;
75   Yet fortune cannot recompense me better
      Than to die well and not my master's debtor.

                    [Exeunt.]

Scene IV

The Forest of Arden.

[Enter ROSALIND *for* GANYMEDE, CELIA *for* ALIENA, *and Clown alias* TOUCHSTONE.*]*

Rosalind
O Jupiter, how weary are my spirits!
Touchstone
I care not for my spirits, if my legs were not weary.
Rosalind
I could find in my heart to disgrace my man's apparel,
and to cry like a woman; but I must comfort the weaker
vessel, as doublet and hose ought to show itself coura-   5
geous to petticoat; therefore, courage, good Aliena.
Celia
I pray you bear with me; I cannot go no further.
Touchstone
For my part, I had rather bear with you than bear you;
yet I should bear no cross if I did bear you; for I think
you have no money in your purse.   10
Rosalind
Well, this is the Forest of Arden.
Touchstone
Ay, now am I in Arden; the more fool I; when I was
at home I was in a better place; but travellers must be
content.

[Enter CORIN *and* SILVIUS.*]*

Rosalind
Ay, be so, good Touchstone. Look you, who comes   15
here, a young man and an old in solemn talk.
Corin
That is the way to make her scorn you still.
Silvius
O Corin, that thou knew'st how I do love her!

Corin
I partly guess; for I have lov'd ere now.
Silvius
20 No, Corin, being old, thou canst not guess,
Though in thy youth thou wast as true a lover
As ever sigh'd upon a midnight pillow.
But if thy love were ever like to mine,
As sure I think did never man love so,
25 How many actions most ridiculous
Hast thou been drawn to by thy fantasy?
Corin
Into a thousand that I have forgotten.
Silvius
O, thou didst then never love so heartily!
If thou rememb'rest not the slightest folly
30 That ever love did make thee run into,
Thou hast not lov'd;
Or if thou hast not sat as I do now,
Wearing thy hearer in thy mistress' praise,
Thou hast not lov'd;
35 Or if thou hast not broke from company
Abruptly, as my passion now makes me,
Thou hast not lov'd.
O Phebe, Phebe, Phebe! *[Exit SILVIUS.]*
Rosalind
Alas, poor shepherd! searching of thy wound,
40 I have by hard adventure found mine own.
Touchstone
And I mine. I remember, when I was in love, I broke
my sword upon a stone, and bid him take that for
coming a-night to Jane Smile; and I remember the
kissing of her batler, and the cow's dugs that her pretty
45 chopt hands had milk'd; and I remember the wooing
of a peascod instead of her; from whom I took two
cods, and, giving her them again, said with weeping
tears 'Wear these for my sake'. We that are true lovers

run into strange capers; but as all is mortal in nature,
so is all nature in love mortal in folly.   50
Rosalind
Thou speak'st wiser than thou art ware of.
Touchstone
Nay, I shall ne'er be ware of mine own wit till I break
my shins against it.
Rosalind
Jove, Jove! this shepherd's passion
Is much upon my fashion.   55
Touchstone
And mine; but it grows something stale with me.
Celia
I pray you, one of you question yond man
If he for gold will give us any food;
I faint almost to death.
Touchstone
Holla, you clown!   60
Rosalind
Peace, fool; he's not thy kinsman.
Corin
Who calls?
Touchstone
Your betters, sir.
Corin
                      Else are they very wretched.
Rosalind
Peace, I say. Good even to you, friend.
Corin
And to you, gentle sir, and to you all.   65
Rosalind
I prithee, shepherd, if that love or gold
Can in this desert place buy entertainment,
Bring us where we may rest ourselves and feed.
Here's a young maid with travel much oppress'd,
And faints for succour.

Corin

70   Fair sir, I pity her,
     And wish, for her sake more than for mine own,
     My fortunes were more able to relieve her;
     But I am shepherd to another man,
     And do not shear the fleeces that I graze.
75   My master is of churlish disposition,
     And little recks to find the way to heaven
     By doing deeds of hospitality.
     Besides, his cote, his flocks, and bounds of feed,
     Are now on sale; and at our sheepcote now,
80   By reason of his absence, there is nothing
     That you will feed on; but what is, come see,
     And in my voice most welcome shall you be.

Rosalind

     What is he that shall buy his flock and pasture?

Corin

     That young swain that you saw here but erewhile,
85   That little cares for buying any thing.

Rosalind

     I pray thee, if it stand with honesty,
     Buy thou the cottage, pasture, and the flock,
     And thou shalt have to pay for it of us.

Celia

     And we will mend thy wages. I like this place,
90   And willingly could waste my time in it.

Corin

     Assuredly the thing is to be sold.
     Go with me; if you like upon report
     The soil, the profit, and this kind of life,
     I will your very faithful feeder be,
95   And buy it with your gold right suddenly.

[Exeunt]

Scene V

Another part of the Forest.

[Enter AMIENS, JAQUES, and Others.]

[Song.]

Amiens
  Under the greenwood tree
  Who loves to lie with me.
  And turn his merry note
  Unto the sweet bird's throat,
Come hither, come hither, come hither.   5
  Here shall he see
  No enemy
But winter and rough weather.

Jaques
More, more, I prithee, more.

Amiens
It will make you melancholy, Monsieur Jaques. 10

Jaques
I thank it. More, I prithee, more. I can suck melancholy
out of a song, as a weasel sucks eggs. More, I prithee,
more.

Amiens
My voice is ragged; I know I cannot please you.

Jaques
I do not desire you to please me; I do desire you to 15
sing. Come, more; another stanzo. Call you 'em
stanzos?

Amiens
What you will, Monsieur Jaques.

Jaques
Nay, I care not for their names; they owe me nothing.
Will you sing? 20

Amiens
More at your request than to please myself.

Jaques

Well then, if ever I thank any man, I'll thank you; but
that they call compliment is like th' encounter of two
dog-apes; and when a man thanks me heartily,
25   methinks I have given him a penny, and he renders
me the beggarly thanks. Come, sing; and you that will
not, hold your tongues.

Amiens

Well, I'll end the song. Sirs, cover the while; the Duke
will drink under this tree. He hath been all this day
30   to look you.

Jaques

And I have been all this day to avoid him. He is too
disputable for my company. I think of as many matters
as he; but I give heaven thanks, and make no boast of
them. Come, warble, come.

[Song.]

35   All together here.

Who doth ambition shun,
And loves to live i' th' sun,
Seeking the food he eats,
And pleas'd with what he gets,
40   Come hither, come hither, come hither.
Here shall he see
No enemy

But winter and rough weather.

Jaques

I'll give you a verse to this note that I made yesterday
45   in despite of my invention.

Amiens

And I'll sing it.

Jaques

Thus it goes:

If it do come to pass
That any man turn ass,

Leaving his wealth and ease 50
A stubborn will to please,

Ducdame, ducdame, ducdame;

Here shall he see
Gross fools as he,

An if he will come to me. 55
Amiens
What's that 'ducdame'?
Jaques
'Tis a Greek invocation, to call fools into a circle. I'll go sleep, if I can; if I cannot, I'll rail against all the first-born of Egypt.
Amiens
And I'll go seek the Duke; his banquet is prepar'd. 60

[Exeunt severally.]

Scene VI

The forest.

[Enter ORLANDO *and* ADAM.*]*

Adam

Dear master, I can go no further. O, I die for food!
Here lie I down, and measure out my grave. Farewell,
kind master.

Orlando

Why, how now, Adam! No greater heart in thee? Live
5   a little; comfort a little; cheer thyself a little. If this
uncouth forest yield anything savage, I will either be
food for it or bring it for food to thee. Thy conceit is
nearer death than thy powers. For my sake be comfort-
able; hold death awhile at the arm's end. I will here
10   be with thee presently; and if I bring thee not something to eat, I will give thee leave to die; but if thou
diest before I come, thou art a mocker of my labour.
Well said! thou look'st cheerly; and I'll be with thee
quickly. Yet thou liest in the bleak air. Come, I will
15   bear thee to some shelter; and thou shalt not die for
lack of a dinner, if there live any thing in this desert.
Cheerly, good Adam!

[Exeunt.]

Scene VII

The forest

[A table set out. Enter DUKE SENIOR, AMIENS, and LORDS, like outlaws.]

Duke Senior
    I think he be transform'd into a beast;
    For I can nowhere find him like a man.
1 Lord
    My lord, he is but even now gone hence;
    Here was he merry, hearing of a song.
Duke Senior
    If he, compact of jars, grow musical,   5
    We shall have shortly discord in the spheres.
    Go seek him; tell him I would speak with him.

[Enter JAQUES.]

1 Lord
    He saves my labour by his own approach.
Duke Senior
    Why, how now, monsieur! what a life is this,
    That your poor friends must woo your company?   10
    What, you look merrily!
Jaques
    A fool, a fool! I met a fool i' th' forest,
    A motley fool. A miserable world!
    As I do live by food, I met a fool,
    Who laid him down and bask'd him in the sun,   15
    And rail'd on Lady Fortune in good terms,
    In good set terms – and yet a motley fool.
    'Good morrow, fool' quoth I; 'No, sir,' quoth he
    'Call me not fool till heaven hath sent me
        fortune.'
    And then he drew a dial from his poke,   20
    And, looking on it with lack-lustre eye,

Says very wisely 'It is ten o'clock;
Thus we may see' quoth he 'how the world wags;
'Tis but an hour ago since it was nine;
25 And after one hour more 'twill be eleven;
And so, from hour to hour, we ripe and ripe,
And then, from hour to hour, we rot and rot;
And thereby hangs a tale'. When I did hear
The motley fool thus moral on the time,
30 My lungs began to crow like chanticleer
That fools should be so deep contemplative;
And I did laugh sans intermission
An hour by his dial. O noble fool!
A worthy fool! Motley's the only wear.

Duke Senior
35 What fool is this?

Jaques
O worthy fool! One that hath been a courtier,
And says, if ladies be but young and fair,
They have the gift to know it; and in his brain,
Which is as dry as the remainder biscuit
40 After a voyage, he hath strange places cramm'd
With observation, the which he vents
In mangled forms. O that I were a fool!
I am ambitious for a motley coat.

Duke Senior
Thou shalt have one.

Jaques
It is my only suit,
45 Provided that your weed your better judgments
Of all opinion that grows rank in them
That I am wise. I must have liberty
Withal, as large a charter as the wind,
To blow on whom I please, for so fools have;
50 And they that are most galled with my folly,
They most must laugh. And why, sir, must they so?
The why is plain as way to parish church:
He that a fool doth very wisely hit

Doth very foolishly, although he smart,
Not to seem senseless of the bob; if not,   55
The wise man's folly is anatomiz'd
Even by the squand'ring glances of the fool.
Invest me in my motley; give me leave
To speak my mind, and I will through and through
Cleanse the foul body of th' infected world,   60
If they will patiently receive my medicine.

Duke Senior
Fie on thee! I can tell what thou wouldst do.

Jaques
What, for a counter, would I do but good?

Duke Senior
Most mischievous foul sin, in chiding sin;
For thou thyself hast been a libertine,   65
As sensual as the brutish sting itself;
And all th'embossed sores and headed evils
That thou with licence of free foot hast caught
Wouldst thou disgorge into the general world.

Jaques
Why, who cries out on pride   70
That can therein tax any private party?
Doth it not flow as hugely as the sea,
Till that the wearer's very means do ebb?
What woman in the city do I name
When that I say the city-woman bears   75
The cost of princes on unworthy shoulders?
Who can come in and say that I mean her,
When such a one as she such is her neighbour?
Or what is he of bases function
That says his bravery is not on my cost,   80
Thinking that I mean him, but therein suits
His folly to the mettle of my speech?
There then! how then? what then? Let me see
    wherein
My tongue hath wrong'd him: if it do him right,
Then he hath wrong'd himself; if he be free,   85

Why then my taxing like a wild-goose flies,
Unclaim'd of any man. But who comes here?

[Enter ORLANDO, with his sword drawn.]

Orlando
Forbear, and eat no more.
Jaques
                              Why, I have eat none yet.
Orlando
Nor shalt not, till necessity be serv'd.
Jaques
90   Of what kind should this cock come of?
Duke Senior
Art thou thus bolden'd, man, by thy distress?
Or else a rude despiser of good manners,
That in civility thou seem'st so empty?
Orlando
You touch'd my vein at first: the thorny point
95   Of bare distress hath ta'en from me the show
Of smooth civility; yet am I inland bred,
And know some nurture. But forbear, I say;
He dies that touches any of this fruit
Till I and my affairs are answered.
Jaques
100   An you will not be answer'd with reason, I must die.
Duke Senior
What would you have? Your gentleness shall force
More than your force move us to gentleness.
Orlando
I almost die for food, and let me have it.
Duke Senior
Sit down and feed, and welcome to our table.
Orlando
105   Speak you so gently? Pardon me, I pray you;
I thought that all things had been savage here,
And therefore put I on the countenance
Of stern commandment. But whate'er you are

That in this desert inaccessible,
Under the shade of melancholy boughs,   110
Lose and neglect the creeping hours of time;
If ever you have look'd on better days,
If ever been where bells have knoll'd to church,
If ever sat at any good man's feast,
If ever from your eyelids wip'd a tear,   115
And know what 'tis to pity and be pitied,
Let gentleness my strong enforcement be;
In the which hope I blush, and hide my sword.
Duke Senior
True is it that we have seen better days,
And have with holy bell been knoll'd to church,   120
And sat at good men's feasts, and wip'd our eyes
Of drops that sacred pity hath engend'red;
And therefore sit you down in gentleness,
And take upon command what help we have
That to your wanting may be minist'red.   125
Orlando
Then but forbear your food a little while,
Whiles, like a doe, I go to find my fawn,
And give it food. There is an old poor man
Who after me hath many a weary step
Limp'd in pure love; till he be first suffic'd,   130
Oppress'd with two weak evils, age and hunger,
I will not touch a bit.
Duke Senior
                  Go find him out.
And we will nothing waste till you return.
Orlando
I thank ye; and be blest for your good comfort!
[Exit.]
Duke Senior
Thou seest we are not all alone unhappy: 135
This wide and universal theatre
Presents more woeful pageants than the scene
Wherein we play in.

Jaques

All the world's a stage,
And all the men and women merely players;
140   They have their exits and their entrances;
And one man in his time plays many parts,
His acts being seven ages. At first the infant,
Mewling and puking in the nurse's arms;
Then the whining school-boy, with his satchel
145   And shining morning face, creeping like snail
Unwillingly to school. And then the lover,
Sighing like furnace, with a woeful ballad
Made to his mistress' eyebrow. Then a soldier,
Full of strange oaths, and bearded like the pard,
150   Jealous in honour, sudden and quick in quarrel,
Seeking the bubble reputation
Even in the cannon's mouth. And then the justice,
In fair round belly with good capon lin'd,
With eyes severe and beard of formal cut,
155   Full of wise saws and modern instances;
And so he plays his part. The sixth age shifts
Into the lean and slipper'd pantaloon,
With spectacles on nose and pouch on side,
His youthful hose, well sav'd, a world too wide
160   For his shrunk shank; and his big manly voice,
Turning again toward childish treble, pipes
And whistles in his sound. Last scene of all,
That ends this strange eventful history,
Is second childishness and mere oblivion;
165   Sans teeth, sans eyes, sans taste, sans every thing.

[Re-enter ORLANDO *with* ADAM.*]*

Duke Senior
Welcome. Set down your venerable burden.
And let him feed.
Orlando
I thank you most for him.

Adam
>   So had you need;
> I scarce can speak to thank you for myself.

Duke Senior
> Welcome; fall to. I will not trouble you   170
> As yet to question you about your fortunes.
> Give us some music; and, good cousin, sing.

[Song.]

>   Blow, blow, thou winter wind,
>   Thou art not so unkind
>   As man's ingratitude;   175
>   Thy tooth is not so keen,
>   Because thou art not seen,
>   Although thy breath be rude.

> Heigh-ho! sing heigh-ho! unto the green holly!
> Most friendship is feigning, most loving mere
>   folly.   180

>   Then, heigh-ho, the holly!
>   This life is most jolly.
>   Freeze, freeze, thou bitter sky,
>   That dost not bite so nigh
>   As benefits forgot;   185
>   Though thou the waters warp,
>   Thy sting is not so sharp

> As friend rememb'red not.
> Heigh-ho! sing, etc.

Duke Senior
> If that you were the good Sir Rowland's son,   190
> As you have whisper'd faithfully you were,
> And as mine eye doth his effigies witness
> Most truly limn'd and living in your face,
> Be truly welcome hither. I am the Duke
> That lov'd your father. The residue of your fortune,   195
> Go to my cave and tell me. Good old man,
> Thou art right welcome as they master is.

Support him by the arm. Give me your hand,
And let me all your fortunes understand.

[Exeunt.]

ACT THREE
Scene I

The palace.

[Enter DUKE FREDERICK, OLIVER, *and* LORDS.*]*

Duke Frederick
Not see him since! Sir, sir, that cannot be.
But were I not the better part made mercy,
I should not seek an absent argument
Of my revenge, thou present. But look to it:
Find out thy brother wheresoe'er he is;   5
Seek him with candle; bring him dead or living
Within this twelvemonth, or turn thou no more
To seek a living in our territory.
Thy lands and all things that thou dost call thine
Worth seizure do we seize into our hands,   10
Till thou canst quit thee by thy brother's mouth
Of what we think against thee.

Oliver
O that your Highness knew my heart in this!
I never lov'd my brother in my life.

Duke Frederick
More villain thou. Well, push him out of doors;   15
And let my officers of such a nature
Make an extent upon his house and lands.
Do this expediently, and turn him going.

[Exeunt.]

Scene II

The forest.

[Enter ORLANDO, with a paper.]

Orlando
Hang there, my verse, in witness of my love;
And thou, thrice-crowned Queen of Night, survey
With thy chaste eye, from thy pale sphere above,
Thy huntress' name that my full life doth sway.
5   O Rosalind! these trees shall be my books,
And in their barks my thoughts I'll character,
That every eye which in this forest looks
Shall see thy virtue witness'd every where.
Run, run, Orlando; carve on every tree,
10   The fair, the chaste, and unexpressive she.

[Exit.]

[Enter CORIN and TOUCHSTONE.]

Corin
And how like you this shepherd's life, Master
Touchstone?

Touchstone
Truly, shepherd, in respect of itself; it is a good life; but
in respect that it is a shepherd's life, it is nought. In
15   respect that it is solitary, I like it very well; but in respect
that it is private, it is a very vile life. Now in respect it
is in the fields, it pleaseth me well; but in respect it is
not in the court, it is tedious. As it is a spare life, look
you, it fits my humour well; but as there is no more
20   plenty in it, it goes much against my stomach. Hast any
philosophy in thee, shepherd?

Corin
No more but that I know the more one sickens the
worse at ease he is; and that he that wants money,
means, and content, is without three good friends; that

the property of rain is to wet, and fire to burn; that 25
good pasture makes fat sheep; and that a great cause
of the night is lack of the sun; that he that hath learned
no wit by nature nor art may complain of good
breeding, or comes of a very dull kindred.

Touchstone

Such a one is a natural philosopher. Wast ever in court, 30
shepherd?

Corin

No, truly.

Touchstone

Then thou art damn'd.

Corin

Nay, I hope.

Touchstone

Truly, thou art damn'd, like an ill-roasted egg, all on
one side. 35

Corin

For not being at court? Your reason.

Touchstone

Why, if thou never wast at court thou never saw'st
good manners; if thou never saw'st good manners,
then thy manners must be wicked; and wickedness is
sin, and sin is damnation. Thou art in a parlous state, 40
shepherd.

Corin

Not a whit, Touchstone. Those that are good manners
at the court are as ridiculous in the country as the
behaviour of the country is most mockable at the court.
You told me you salute not at the court, but you kiss 45
your hands; that courtesy would be uncleanly if
courtiers were shepherds.

Touchstone

Instance, briefly; come, instance.

Corin

Why, we are still handling our ewes; and their fells,
you know, are greasy. 50

Touchstone

Why, do not your courtier's hands sweat? And is not the grease of a mutton as wholesome as the sweat of a man? Shallow, shallow. A better instance, I say; come.

Corin

Besides, our hands are hard.

Touchstone

55 Your lips will feel them the sooner. Shallow again. A more sounder instance; come.

Corin

And they are often tarr'd over with the surgery of our sheep; and would you have us kiss tar? The courtier's hands are perfum'd with civet.

Touchstone

60 Most shallow man! thou worm's meat in respect of a good piece of flesh indeed! Learn of the wise, and perpend: civet is of a baser birth than tar – the very uncleanly flux of a cat. Mend the instance, shepherd.

Corin

65 You have too courtly a wit for me; I'll rest.

Touchstone

Wilt thou rest damn'd? God help thee, shallow man! God make incision in thee! thou art raw.

Corin

Sir, I am a true labourer: I earn that I eat, get that I wear; owe no man hate, envy no man's happiness;

70 glad of other men's good, content with my harm; and the greatest of my pride is to see my ewes graze and my lambs suck.

Touchstone

That is another simple sin in you: to bring the ewes and the rams together, and to offer to get your living

75 by the copulation of cattle; to be bawd to a bell-wether, and to betray a she-lamb of a twelvemonth to a crooked-pated, old, cuckoldly ram, out of all reasonable match. If thou beest not damn'd for this, the devil

himself will have no shepherds; I cannot see else how
thou shouldst scape.   80
Corin
Here comes young Master Ganymede, my new
mistress's brother.

[Enter ROSALIND, reading a paper.]

Rosalind
    'From the east to western Inde,
    No jewel is like Rosalinde.
    Her worth, being mounted on the wind,   15
    Through all the world bears
    Rosalinde.
    All the pictures fairest lin'd
    Are but black to Rosalinde.
    Let no face be kept in mind   90
    But the fair of Rosalinde.'
Touchstone
I'll rhyme you so eight years together, dinners, and
suppers, and sleeping hours, excepted. It is the right
butter-women's rank to market.
Rosalind
Out, fool!   95
Touchstone
    For a taste:
    If a hart do lack a hind,
    Let him seek out Rosalinde.
    If the cat will after kind,
    So be sure will Rosalinde.   100
    Winter garments must be lin'd,
    So must slender Rosalinde.
    They that reap must sheaf and bind,
    Then to cart with Rosalinde.
    Sweetest nut hath sourest rind,   105
    Such a nut is Rosalinde.
    He that sweetest rose will find
    Must find love's prick and Rosalinde.

This is the very false gallop of verses; why do you
    intect yourself with them?

Rosalind

110   Peace, you dull fool! I found them on a tree.

Touchstone

Truly, the tree yields bad fruit.

Rosalind

I'll graff it with you, and then I shall graff it with a
medlar. Then it will be the earliest fruit i' th' country;
or you'll be rotten ere you be half ripe, and that's the
115   right virtue of the medlar.

Touchstone

You have said; but whether wisely or no, let the forest
judge.

[Enter CELIA, with a writing.]

Rosalind

Peace!

Here comes my sister, reading; stand aside.

Celia

120   'Why should this a desert be?
          For it is unpeopled? No;
      Tongues I'll hang on every tree
          That shall civil sayings show.
      Some, how brief the life of man
125   Runs his erring pilgrimage,
      That the stretching of a span
          Buckles in his sum of age;
      Some, of violated vows
          'Twixt the souls of friend and friend;
130   But upon the fairest boughs,
          Or at every sentence end,
      Will I Rosalinda write,
          Teaching all that read to know
      The quintessence of every sprite
135   Heaven would in little show.
      Therefore heaven Nature charg'd

That one body should be fill'd
With all graces wide-enlarg'd.
 Nature presently distill'd
Helen's cheek, but not her heart,   140
 Cleopatra's majesty,
Atalanta's better part,
 Sad Lucretia's modesty.
Thus Rosalinde of many parts
 By heavenly synod was devis'd,   145
Of many faces, eyes, and hearts,
 To have the touches dearest priz'd.
Heaven would that she these gifts should
 have,
And I to live and die her slave.'

Rosalind

O most gentle pulpiter! What tedious homily of love 150
have you wearied your parishioners withal, and never
cried 'Have patience, good people'.

Celia

How now! Back, friends; shepherd, go off a little; go
with him, sirrah.

Touchstone

Come, shepherd, let us make an honourable retreat; 155
though not with bag and baggage, yet with scrip and
scrippage.

[Exeunt CORIN *and* TOUCHSTONE.*]*

Celia

Didst thou hear these verses?

Rosalind

O, yes, I heard them all, and more too; for some of
them had in them more feet than the verses would 160
bear.

Celia

That's no matter; the feet might bear the verses.

Rosalind

Ay, but the feet were lame, and could not bear

themselves without the verse, and therefore stood
165 lamely in the verse.

Celia

But didst thou hear without wondering how thy name
should be hang'd and carved upon these trees?

Rosalind

I was seven of the nine days out of the wonder before
you came; for look here what I found on a palm-tree.
170 I was never so berhym'd since Pythagoras' time that I
was an Irish rat, which I can hardly remember.

Celia

Trow you who hath done this?

Rosalind

Is it a man?

Celia

And a chain, that you once wore, about his neck.
175 Change you colour?

Rosalind

I prithee, who?

Celia

O Lord, Lord! it is a hard matter for friends to meet;
but mountains may be remov'd with earthquakes, and
so encounter.

Rosalind

180 Nay, but who is it?

Celia

Is it possible?

Rosalind

Nay, I prithee now, with most petitionary vehemence,
tell me who it is.

Celia

O wonderful, wonderful, and most wonderful
185 wonderful, and yet again wonderful, and after that,
out of all whooping!

Rosalind

Good my complexion! dost thou think, though I am
caparison'd like a man, I have a doublet and hose in

my disposition? One inch of delay more is a South Sea
of discovery. I prithee tell me who is it quickly, and 190
speak apace. I would thou couldst stammer, that thou
mightst pour this conceal'd man out of thy mouth, as
wine comes out of a narrow-mouth'd bottle – either
too much at once or none at all. I prithee take the
cork out of thy mouth that I may drink thy tidings.   195

Celia

So you may put a man in your belly.

Rosalind

Is he of God's making? What manner of man? Is his
head worth a hat or his chin worth a beard?

Celia

Nay, he hath but a little beard.

Rosalind

Why, God will send more if the man will be thankful. 200
Let me stay the growth of his beard, if thou delay me
not the knowledge of his chin.

Celia

It is young Orlando, that tripp'd up the wrestler's heels
and your heart both in an instant.

Rosalind

Nay, but the devil take mocking!   205
Speak sad brow and true maid.

Celia

I' faith, coz, 'tis he.

Rosalind

Orlando?

Celia

Orlando.

Rosalind

Alas the day! what shall I do with my doublet and 210
hose? What did he when thou saw'st him? What said
he? How look'd he? Wherein went he? What makes
he here? Did he ask for me? Where remains he? How
parted he with thee? And when shalt thou see him
again? Answer me in one word.   215

Celia

You must borrow me Gargantua's mouth first; 'tis a word too great for any mouth of this age's size. To say ay and no to these particulars is more than to answer in a catechism.

Rosalind

220 But doth he know that I am in this forest, and in man's apparel? Looks he as freshly as he did the day he wrestled?

Celia

It is as easy to count atomies as to resolve the propositions of a lover; but take a taste of my finding him,
225 and relish it with good observance. I found him under a tree, like a dropp'd acorn.

Rosalind

It may well be call'd Jove's tree, when it drops forth such fruit.

Celia

Give me audience, good madam.

Rosalind

230 Proceed.

Celia

There lay he, stretch'd along like a wounded knight.

Rosalind

Though it be pity to see such a sight, it well becomes the ground.

Celia

Cry 'Holla' to thy tongue, I prithee; it curvets unsea-
235 sonably. He was furnish'd like a hunter.

Rosalind

O, ominous! he comes to kill my heart.

Celia

I would sing my song without a burden; thou bring'st me out of tune.

Rosalind

Do you not know I am a woman?
240 When I think, I must speak. Sweet, say on.

Celia

You bring me out. Soft! comes he not here?

[Enter ORLANDO *and* JAQUES.]

Rosalind

'Tis he; slink by, and note him.

Jaques

I thank you for your company; but, good faith, I had as lief have been myself alone.

Orlando

And so had I; but yet, for fashion sake, I thank you 245 too for your society.

Jaques

God buy you; let's meet as little as we can.

Orlando

I do desire we may be better strangers.

Jaques

I pray you mar no more trees with writing love songs in their barks. 250

Orlando

I pray you mar no moe of my verses with reading them ill-favouredly.

Jaques

Rosalind is your love's name?

Orlando

Yes, just.

Jaques

I do not like her name. 255

Orlando

There was no thought of pleasing you when she was christen'd.

Jaques

What stature is she of?

Orlando

Just as high as my heart.

Jaques

You are full of pretty answers. Have you not been 260

acquainted with goldsmiths' wives, and conn'd them out of rings?

Orlando

Not so; but I answer you right painted cloth, from whence you have studied your questions.

Jaques

265 You have a nimble wit; I think 'twas made of Atalanta's heels. Will you sit down with me? and we two will rail against our mistress the world, and all our misery.

Orlando

I will chide no breather in the world but myself, against whom I know most faults.

Jaques

270 The worst fault you have is to be in love.

Orlando

'Tis a fault I will not change for your best virtue. I am weary of you.

Jaques

By my troth, I was seeking for a fool when I found you.

Orlando

275 He is drown'd in the brook; look but in, and you shall see him.

Jaques

There I shall see mine own figure.

Orlando

Which I take to be either a fool or a cipher.

Jaques

I'll tarry no longer with you; farewell, good Signior
280 Love.

Orlando

I am glad of your departure; adieu, good Monsieur Melancholy.

[Exit JAQUES.*]*

Rosalind

[Aside to CELIA*]* I will speak to him like a saucy lackey,

and under that habit play the knave with him – Do
you hear, forester? 285

Orlando

Very well; what would you?

Rosalind

I pray you, what is't o'clock?

Orlando

You should ask me what time o' day; there's no clock
in the forest.

Rosalind

Then there is no true lover in the forest, else sighing 290
every minute and groaning every hour would detect
the lazy foot of Time as well as a clock.

Orlando

And why not the swift foot of Time?
Had not that been as proper?

Rosalind

By no means, sir. Time travels in divers paces with 295
divers persons. I'll tell you who Time ambles withal,
who Time trots withal, who Time gallops withal, and
who he stands still withal.

Orlando

I prithee, who doth he trot withal?

Rosalind

Marry, he trots hard with a young maid between the 300
contract of her marriage and the day it is solemniz'd;
if the interim be but a se'nnight, Time's pace is so hard
that it seems the length of seven year.

Orlando

Who ambles Time withal?

Rosalind

With a priest that lacks Latin and a rich man that hath 305
not the gout; for the one sleeps easily because he cannot
study, and the other lives merrily because he feels no
pain; the one lacking the burden of lean and wasteful
learning, the other knowing not burden of heavy
tedious penury. These Time ambles withal. 310

Orlando

ho doth he gallop withal?

Rosalind

With a thief to the gallows; for though he go as softly
as foot can fall, he thinks himself too soon there.

Orlando

Who stays it still withal?

Rosalind

315   With lawyers in the vacation; for they sleep between
term and term, and then they perceive not how Time
moves.

Orlando

Where dwell you, pretty youth?

Rosalind

With this shepherdess, my sister; here in the skirts of
320   the forest, like fringe upon a petticoat.

Orlando

Are you native of this place?

Rosalind

As the coney that you see dwell where she is kindled.

Orlando

Your accent is something finer than you could purchase
in so removed a dwelling.

Rosalind

325   I have been told so of many; but indeed an old religious uncle of mine taught me to speak, who was in
his youth an inland man; one that knew courtship
too well, for there he fell in love. I have heard him
read many lectures against it; and I thank God I am
330   not a woman, to be touch'd with so many giddy
offences as he hath generally tax'd their whole sex
withal.

Orlando

Can you remember any of the principal evils that he
laid to the charge of women?

Rosalind

335   There were none principal; they were all like one

another as halfpence are; every one fault seeming monstrous till his fellow-fault came to match it.

Orlando

I prithee recount some of them.

Rosalind

No; I will not cast away my physic but on those that are sick. There is a man haunts the forest that abuses 340 our young plants with carving 'Rosalind' on their barks; hangs odes upon hawthorns and elegies on brambles; all, forsooth, deifying the name of Rosalind. If I could meet that fancy-monger, I would give him some good counsel, for he seems to have the quotidian of love 345 upon him.

Orlando

I am he that is so love-shak'd; I pray you tell me your remedy.

Rosalind

There is none of my uncle's marks upon you; he taught me how to know a man in love; in which cage of 350 rushes I am sure you are not prisoner.

Orlando

What were his marks?

Rosalind

A lean cheek, which you have not; a blue eye and sunken, which you have not; an unquestionable spirit, which you have not; a beard neglected, which you have not; but I 355 pardon you for that, for simply your having in beard is a younger brother's revenue. Then your hose should be ungarter'd, your bonnet unbanded, your sleeve unbutton'd, your shoe untied, and every thing about you demonstrating a careless desolation. But you are no such 360 man; you are rather point-device in your accoutrements, as loving yourself than seeming the lover of any other.

Orlando

Fair youth, I would I could make thee believe I love.

Rosalind

Me believe it! You may as soon make her that you love

365   believe it; which, I warrant, she is apter to do than to confess she does. That is one of the points in the which women still give the lie to their consciences. But, in good sooth, are you he that hangs the verses on the trees wherein Rosalind is so admired?

Orlando

370   I swear to thee, youth, by the white hand of Rosalind, I am that he, that unfortunate he.

Rosalind

But are you so much in love as your rhymes speak?

Orlando

Neither rhyme nor reason can express how much.

Rosalind

Love is merely a madness; and, I tell you, deserves as
375   well a dark house and a whip as madmen do; and the reason why they are not so punish'd and cured is that the lunacy is so ordinary that the whippers are in love too. Yet I profess curing it by counsel.

Orlando

Did you ever cure any so?

Rosalind

380   Yes, one; and in this manner. He was to imagine me his love, his mistress; and I set him every day to woo me; at which time would I, being but a moonish youth, grieve, be effeminate, changeable, longing and liking, proud, fantastical, apish, shallow, inconstant, full of
385   tears, full of smiles; for every passion something and for no passion truly anything, as boys and women are for the most part cattle of this colour; would now like him, now loathe him; then entertain him, then forswear him; now weep for him, then spit at him; that I drave
390   my suitor from his mad humour of love to a living humour of madness; which was, to forswear the full stream of the world and to live in a nook merely monastic. And thus I cur'd him; and this way will I take upon me to wash your liver as clean as a sound sheep's
395   heart, that there shall not be one spot of love in 't.

Orlando

I would not be cured, youth.

Rosalind

I would cure you, if you would but call me Rosalind,
and come every day to my cote and woo me.

Orlando

Now, by the faith of my love, I will. Tell me where it
is.   400

Rosalind

Go with me to it, and I'll show it you; and, by the
way, you shall tell me where in the forest you live.
Will you go?

Orlando

With all my heart, good youth.

Rosalind

Nay, you must call me Rosalind.   405
Come, sister, will you go?

[Exeunt.]

Scene III

The forest.

[Enter TOUCHSTONE *and* AUDREY; JAQUES *behind.]*

Touchstone
 Come apace, good Audrey; I will fetch up your goats,
 Audrey. And how, Audrey, am I the man yet? Doth
 my simple feature content you?
Audrey
 Your features! Lord warrant us! What features?
Touchstone
5 I am here with thee and thy goats, as the most capri-
 cious poet, honest Ovid, was among the Goths.
Jaques
 [Aside] O knowledge ill-inhabited, worse than Jove in
 a thatch'd house!
Touchstone
 When a man's verses cannot be understood, nor a
10 man's good wit seconded with the forward child under-
 standing, it strikes a man more dead than a great
 reckoning in a little room. Truly, I would the gods had
 made thee poetical.
Audrey
 I do not know what 'poetical' is. Is it honest in deed
15 and word? Is it a true thing?
Touchstone
 No, truly; for the truest poetry is the most feigning,
 and lovers are given to poetry; and what they swear
 in poetry may be said as lovers they do feign.
Audrey
 Do you wish, then, that the gods had made me
20 poetical?
Touchstone
 I do, truly, for thou swear'st to me thou art honest;
 now, if thou wert a poet, I might have some hope thou
 didst feign.

Audrey

Would you not have me honest?

Touchstone

No, truly, unless thou wert hard-favour'd; for honesty   25
coupled to beauty is to have honey a sauce to sugar.

Jaques

[Aside] A material fool!

Audrey

Well, I am not fair; and therefore I pray the gods make
me honest.

Touchstone

Truly, and to cast away honesty upon a foul slut were   30
to put good meat into an unclean dish.

Audrey

I am not a slut, though I thank the gods I am foul.

Touchstone

Well, praised be the gods for thy foulness; sluttishness
may come hereafter. But be it as it may be, I will marry
thee; and to that end I have been with Sir Oliver   35
Martext, the vicar of the next village, who hath
promis'd to meet me in this place of the forest, and
to couple us.

Jaques

[Aside] I would fain see this meeting.

Audrey

Well, the gods give us joy!   40

Touchstone

Amen. A man may, if he were of a fearful heart, stagger
in this attempt; for here we have no temple but the
wood, no assembly but horn-beasts. But what though?
Courage! As horns are odious, they are necessary. It is
said: 'Many a man knows no end of his goods'. Right!   45
Many a man has good horns and knows no end of
them. Well, that is the dowry of his wife; 'tis none of
his own getting. Horns? Even so. Poor men alone? No,
no; the noblest deer hath them as huge as the rascal.
Is the single man therefore blessed? No; as a wall'd   50

town is more worthier than a village, so is the forehead
of a married man more honourable than the bare brow
of a bachelor; and by how much defence is better than
no skill, by so much is a horn more precious than to
55   want. Here comes Sir Oliver.

[Enter SIR OLIVER MARTEXT.]*

Sir Oliver Martext, you are well met. Will you dispatch
us here under this tree, or shall we go with you to
your chapel?

Sir Oliver

Is there none here to give the woman?

Touchstone

60   I will not take her on gift of any man.

Sir Oliver

Truly, she must be given, or the marriage is not lawful.

Jaques

[Discovering himself] Proceed, proceed; I'll give her.

Touchstone

Good even, good Master What-ye-call't; how do you,
sir? You are very well met. Goddild you for your last
65   company. I am very glad to see you. Even a toy in
hand here, sir. Nay; pray be cover'd.

Jaques

Will you be married, motley?

Touchstone

As the ox hath his bow, sir, the horse his curb, and
the falcon her bells, so man hath his desires; and as
70   pigeons bill, so wedlock would be nibbling.

Jaques

And will you, being a man of your breeding, be married
under a bush, like a beggar? Get you to church and
have a good priest that can tell you what marriage is;
this fellow will but join you together as they join
75   wainscot; then one of you will prove a shrunk panel,
and like green timber warp, warp.

Touchstone
    [Aside] I am not in the mind but I were better to be
    married of him than of another; for he is not like to
    marry me well; and not being well married, it will be
    a good excuse for me hereafter to leave my wife.   80
Jaques
    Go thou with me, and let me counsel thee.
Touchstone
    Come, sweet Audrey;
    We must be married or we must live in bawdry.
    Farewell, good Master Oliver. Not –

        O sweet Oliver,   85
        O brave Oliver,
      Leave me not behind thee.
        But –
        Wind away,
        Begone, I say,   90
      I will not to wedding with thee.

    [Exeunt JAQUES, TOUCHSTONE, *and* AUDREY.*]*

Sir Oliver
    'Tis no matter; ne'er a fantastical knave of them all
    shall flout me out of my calling.

    [Exit.]

Scene IV

The forest.

[Enter ROSALIND *and* CELIA.*]*

Rosalind
Never talk to me; I will weep.

Celia
Do, I prithee; but yet have the grace to consider that tears do not become a man.

Rosalind
But have I not cause to weep?

Celia
5   As good cause as one would desire; therefore weep.

Rosalind
His very hair is of the dissembling colour.

Celia
Something browner than Judas's. Marry, his kisses are Judas's own children.

Rosalind
I'faith, his hair is of a good colour.

Celia
10   An excellent colour: your chestnut was ever the only colour.

Rosalind
And his kissing is as full of sanctity as the touch of holy bread.

Celia
He hath bought a pair of cast lips of Diana. A nun of
15   winter's sisterhood kisses not more religiously; the very ice of chastity is in them.

Rosalind
But why did he swear he would come this morning, and comes not?

Celia
Nay, certainly, there is no truth in him.

Rosalind

Do you think so? 20

Celia

Yes; I think he is not a pick-purse nor a horse-stealer;
but for his verity in love, I do think him as concave
as a covered goblet or a worm-eaten nut.

Rosalind

Not true in love?

Celia

Yes, when is he in, but I think he is not in. 25

Rosalind

You have heard him swear downright he was.

Celia.

'Was' is not 'is'; besides, the oath of a lover is no
stronger than the word of a tapster; they are both the
confirmer of false reckonings. He attends here in the
forest on the Duke, your father. 30

Rosalind

I met the Duke yesterday, and had much question with
him. He asked me of what parentage I was; I told him,
of as good as he; so he laugh'd and let me go. But
what talk we of fathers when there is such a man as
Orlando? 35

Celia

O, that's a brave man! He writes brave verses, speaks
brave words, swears brave oaths, and breaks them
bravely, quite traverse, athwart the heart of his lover;
as a puny tilter, that spurs his horse but on one side,
breaks his staff like a noble goose. But all's brave that 40
youth mounts and folly guides. Who comes here?

[Enter CORIN.]

Corin

Mistress and master, you have oft enquired
After the shepherd that complain'd of love,
Who you saw sitting by me on the turf,

45   Praising the proud disdainful shepherdess
      That was his mistress.

Celia

                          Well, and what of him?

Corin

      If you will see a pageant truly play'd
      Between the pale complexion of true love
      And the red glow of scorn and proud disdain,
50   Go hence a little, and I shall conduct you,
      If you will mark it.

Rosalind

                 O, come, let us remove!
      The sight of lovers feedeth those in love.
      Bring us to this sight, and you shall say
      I'll prove a busy actor in their play.

            [Exeunt.]

Scene V

Another part of the forest.

[Enter SILVIUS and PHEBE.]

Silvius

Sweet Phebe, do not scorn me; do not, Phebe.
Say that you love me not; but say not so
In bitterness. The common executioner,
Whose heart th' accustom'd sight of death makes
    hard,
Falls not the axe upon the humbled neck   5
But first begs pardon. Will you sterner be
Than he that dies and lives by bloody drops?

[Enter ROSALIND, CELIA, and CORIN, at a distance.]

Phebe

I would not be thy executioner;
I fly thee, for I would not injure thee.
Thou tell'st me there is murder in mine eye.   10
'Tis pretty, sure, and very probable,
That eyes, that are the frail'st and softest things,
Who shut their coward gates on atomies,
Should be call'd tyrants, butchers, murderers!
Now I do frown on thee with all my heart;   15
And if mine eyes can wound, now let them kill thee.
Now counterfeit to swoon; why, now fall down;
Or, if thou canst not, O, for shame, for shame,
Lie not, to say mine eyes are murderers.
Now show the wound mine eye hath made in thee.   20
Scratch thee but with a pin, and there remains
Some scar of it; lean upon a rush,
The cicatrice and capable impressure
Thy palm some moment keeps; but now mine eyes,
Which I have darted at thee, hurt thee not;   25
Nor, I am sure, there is not force in eyes
That can do hurt.

Silvius
                    O dear Phebe,
    If ever – as that ever may be near –
    You meet in some fresh cheek the power of fancy,
30 Then shall you know the wounds invisible
    That love's keen arrows make.

Phebe
                                But till that time
    Come not thou near me; and when that time comes,
    Afflict me with thy mocks, pity me not;
    As till that time I shall not pity thee.

Rosalind
    [Advancing] And why, I pray you?
35   Who might be your mother,
    That you insult, exult, and all at once,
    Over the wretched? What though you have no
        beauty –
    As, by my faith, I see no more in you
    Than without candle may go dark to bed –
40 Must you be therefore proud and pitiless?
    Why, what means this? Why do you look on me?
    I see no more in you than in the ordinary
    Of nature's sale-work. 'Od's my little life,
    I think she means to tangle my eyes too!
45 No, faith, proud mistress, hope not after it;
    'Tis not your inky brows, your black silk hair,
    Your bugle eyeballs, nor your cheek of cream,
    That can entame my spirits to your worship.
    You foolish shepherd, wherefore do you follow her,
50 Like foggy south, puffing with wind and rain?
    You are a thousand times a properer man
    Than she a woman. 'Tis such fools as you
    That makes the world full of ill-favour'd children.
    'Tis not her glass, but you, that flatters her;
55 And out of you she sees herself more proper
    Than any of her lineaments can show her.
    But, mistress, know yourself. Down on your knees,

And thank heaven, fasting, for a good man's love;
For I must tell you friendly in your ear:
Sell when you can; you are not for all markets.   60
Cry the man mercy, love him, take his offer;
Foul is most foul, being foul to be a scoffer.
So take her to thee, shepherd. Fare you well.

Phebe

Sweet youth, I pray you chide a year together;
I had rather hear you chide than this man woo.   65

Rosalind

He's fall'n in love with your foulness, and she'll fall
in love with my anger. If it be so, as fast as she answers
thee with frowning looks, I'll sauce her with bitter
words. Why look you so upon me?

Phebe

For no ill will I bear you.   70

Rosalind

I pray you do not fall in love with me,
For I am falser than vows made in wine;
Besides, I like you not. If you will know my house,
'Tis at the tuft of olives here hard by.
Will you go, sister? Shepherd, ply her hard.   75
Come, sister. Shepherdess, look on him better,
And be not proud; though all the world could see,
None could be so abus'd in sight as he.
Come, to our flock.

[Exeunt ROSALIND, CELIA, and CORIN.]

Phebe

Dead shepherd, now I find thy saw of might: 80
'Who ever lov'd that lov'd not at first sight?'

Silvius

Sweet Phebe.

Phebe

       Ha! What say'st thou, Silvius?

Silvius

Sweet Phebe, pity me.

Phebe
Why, I am sorry for thee, gentle Silvius.
Silvius
85   Wherever sorrow is, relief would be.
If you do sorrow at my grief in love,
By giving love, your sorrow and my grief
Were both extermin'd.
Phebe
Thou hast my love; is not that neighbourly?
Silvius
I would have you.
Phebe
90   Why, that were covetousness.
Silvius, the time was that I hated thee;
And yet it is not that I bear thee love;
But since that thou canst talk of love so well,
Thy company, which erst was irksome to me,
95   I will endure; and I'll employ thee too.
But do not look for further recompense
Than thine own gladness that thou art employ'd
Silvius
So holy and so perfect is my love,
And I in such a poverty of grace,
100   That I shall think it a most plenteous crop
To glean the broken ears after the man
That the main harvest reaps; loose now and then
A scatt'red smile, and that I'll live upon.
Phebe
Know'st thou the youth that spoke to me erewhile?
Silvius
105   Not very well; but I have met him oft;
And he hath bought the cottage and the bounds
That the old carlot once was master of.
Phebe
Think not I love him, though I ask for him;
'Tis but a peevish boy; yet he talks well.
110   But what care I for words? Yet words do well

When he that speaks them pleases those that hear.
It is a pretty youth – not very pretty;
But, sure, he's proud; and yet his pride becomes
   him.
He'll make a proper man. The best thing in him
Is his complexion; and faster than his tongue   115
Did make offence, his eye did heal it up.
He is not very tall; yet for his years he's tall;
His leg is but so-so; and yet 'tis well.
There was a pretty redness in his lip,
A little riper and more lusty red   120
Than that mix'd in his cheek; 'twas just the
   difference
Betwixt the constant red and mingled damask.
There be some women, Silvius, had they mark'd him
In parcels as I did, would have gone near
To fall in love with him; but, for my part,   125
I love him not, nor hate him not; and yet
I have more cause to hate him than to love him;
For what had he to do to chide at me?
He said mine eyes were black, and my hair black,
And, now I am rememb'red, scorn'd at me.   130
I marvel why I answer'd not again;
But that's all one: omittance is no quittance.
I'll write to him a very taunting letter,
And thou shalt bear it; wilt thou, Silvius?
Silvius
   Phebe, with all my heart.
Phebe
                  I'll write it straight;   135
The matter's in my head and in my heart;
I will be bitter with him and passing short.
Go with me, Silvius.

[Exeunt.]

ACT FOUR

Scene I

The forest.

[Enter ROSALIND, CELIA, *and* JAQUES.]

Jaques

I prithee, pretty youth, let me be better acquainted
with thee.

Rosalind

They say you are a melancholy fellow.

Jaques

I am so; I do love it better than laughing.

Rosalind

5   Those that are in extremity of either are abominable
fellows, and betray themselves to every modern censure
worse than drunkards.

Jaques

Why, 'tis good to be sad and say nothing.

Rosalind

Why then, 'tis good to be a post.

Jaques

10   I have neither the scholar's melancholy, which is emula-
tion; nor the musician's, which is fantastical; nor the
courtier's, which is proud; nor the soldier's, which is
ambitious; nor the lawyer's, which is politic; nor the
lady's, which is nice; nor the lover's, which is all these;
15   but it is a melancholy of mine own, compounded of
many simples, extracted from many objects, and, indeed,
the sundry contemplation of my travels; in which my
often rumination wraps me in a most humorous sadness.

Rosalind

A traveller! By my faith, you have great reason to be
20   sad. I fear you have sold your own lands to see other
men's; then to have seen much and to have nothing
is to have rich eyes and poor hands.

Jaques

Yes, I have gain'd my experience.

[Enter ORLANDO.*]*

Rosalind

And your experience makes you sad. I had rather have
a fool to make me merry than experience to make me   25
sad – and to travel for it too.

Orlando

Good day, and happiness, dear Rosalind!

Jaques

Nay, then, God buy you, an you talk in blank verse.

Rosalind

Farewell, Monsieur Traveller; look you lisp and wear
strange suits, disable all the benefits of your own   30
country, be out of love with your nativity, and almost
chide God for making you that countenance you are;
or I will scarce think you have swam in a gondola.
[Exit JAQUES*]* Why, how now, Orlando! where have you
been all this while? You a lover! An you serve me such   35
another trick, never come in my sight more.

Orlando

My fair Rosalind, I come within an hour of my promise.

Rosalind

Break an hour's promise in love! He that will divide
a minute into a thousand parts, and break but a
part of the thousand part of a minute in the affairs   40
of love, it may be said of him that Cupid hath
clapp'd him o' th' shoulder, but I'll warrant him
heart-whole.

Orlando

Pardon me, dear Rosalind.

Rosalind

Nay, an you be so tardy, come no more in my sight.   45
I had as lief be woo'd of a snail.

Orlando

Of a snail!

Rosalind

Ay, of a snail; for though he comes slowly, he carries
his house on his head – a better jointure, I think, than
50 you make a woman; besides, he brings his destiny with
him.

Orlando

What's that?

Rosalind

Why, horns; which such as you are fain to be beholding
to your wives for; but he comes armed in his fortune,
55 and prevents the slander of his wife.

Orlando

Virtue is no horn-maker; and my Rosalind is virtuous.

Rosalind

And I am your Rosalind.

Celia

It pleases him to call you so; but he hath a Rosalind
of a better leer than you.

Rosalind

60 Come, woo me, woo me; for now I am in a holiday
humour, and like enough to consent. What would you
say to me now, an I were your very very rosalind?

Orlando

I would kiss before I spoke.

Rosalind

Nay, you were better speak first; and when you were
65 gravell'd for lack of matter, you might take occasion
to kiss. Very good orators, when they are out, they will
spit; and for lovers lacking – God warn us! – matter,
the cleanliest shift is to kiss.

Orlando

How if the kiss be denied?

Rosalind

70 Then she puts you to entreaty, and there begins new
matter.

Orlando

Who could be out, being before his beloved mistress?

Rosalind

Marry, that should you, if I were your mistress; or I should think my honesty ranker than my wit.

Orlando

What, of my suit? 75

Rosalind

Not out of your apparel, and yet out of your suit. Am not I your Rosalind?

Orlando

I take some joy to say you are, because I would be talking of her.

Rosalind

Well, in her person, I say I will not have you. 80

Orlando

Then, in mine own person, I die.

Rosalind

No, faith, die by attorney. The poor world is almost six thousand years old, and in all this time there was not any man died in his own person, videlicet, in a love-cause. Troilus had his brains dash'd out with a 85 Grecian club; yet he did what he could to die before, and he is one of the patterns of love. Leander, he would have liv'd many a fair year, though Hero had turn'd nun, if it had not been for a hot midsummer-night; for, good youth, he went but forth to wash him 90 in the Hellespont, and, being taken with the cramp, was drown'd; and the foolish chroniclers of that age found it was – Hero of Sestos. But these are all lies: men have died from time to time, and worms have eaten them, but not for love. 95

Orlando

I would not have my right Rosalind of this mind; for, I protest, her frown might kill me.

Rosalind

By this hand, it will not kill a fly. But come, now I will be your Rosalind in a more coming-on disposition; and ask me what you will, I will grant it. 100

Orlando
Then love me, Rosalind.

Rosalind
Yes, faith, will I, Fridays and Saturdays, and all.

Orlando
And wilt thou have me?

Rosalind
Ay, and twenty such.

Orlando
105   What sayest thou?

Rosalind
Are you not good?

Orlando
I hope so.

Rosalind
Why then, can one desire too much of a good thing?
Come, sister, you shall be the priest, and marry us.
110   Give me your hand, Orlando. What do you say, sister?

Orlando
Pray thee, marry us.

Celia
I cannot say the words.

Rosalind
You must begin 'Will you, Orlando' –

Celia
Go to. Will you, Orlando, have to wife this Rosalind?

Orlando
115   I will.

Rosalind
Ay, but when?

Orlando
Why, now; as fast as she can marry us.

Rosalind
Then you must say 'I take thee, Rosalind, for wife'.

Orlando
I take thee, Rosalind, for wife.

Rosalind
    I might ask you for your commission; but – I do take 120
    thee, Orlando, for my husband. There's a girl goes
    before the priest; and, certainly, a woman's thought
    runs before her actions.

Orlando
    So do all thoughts; they are wing'd

Rosalind
    Now tell me how long you would have her, after you 125
    have possess'd her.

Orlando
    For ever and a day.

Rosalind
    Say 'a day' without the 'ever'. No, no,Orlando; men
    are April when they woo, December when they wed:
    maids are May when they are maids, but the sky 130
    changes when they are wives. I will be more jealous
    of thee than a Barbary cock-pigeon over his hen, more
    clamorous than a parrot against rain, more new-fangled
    than an ape, more giddy in my desires than a monkey.
    I will weep for nothing, like Diana in the fountain, 135
    and I will do that when you are dispos'd to be merry;
    I will laugh like a hyen, and that when thou art inclin'd
    to sleep.

Orlando
    But will my Rosalind do so?

Rosalind
    By my life, she will do as I do.   140

Orlando
    O, but she is wise.

Rosalind
    Or else she could not have the wit to do this. The
    wiser, the waywarder. Make the doors upon a woman's
    wit, and it will out at the casement; shut that, and
    'twill out at the key-hole; stop that, 'twill fly with the 145
    smoke out at the chimney.

Orlando

A man that had a wife with such a wit, he might say 'Wit, whither wilt?'

Rosalind

150 Nay, you might keep that check for it, till you met your wife's wit going to your neighbour's bed.

Orlando

And what wit could wit have to excuse that?

Rosalind

Marry, to say she came to seek you there. You shall never take her without her answer, unless you take her without her tongue. O, that woman that cannot 155 make her fault her husband's occasion, let her never nurse her child herself, for she will breed it like a fool!

Orlando

For these two hours, Rosalind, I will leave thee.

Rosalind

Alas, dear love, I cannot lack thee two hours!

Orlando

160 I must attend the Duke at dinner; by two o'clock I will be with thee again.

Rosalind

Ay, go your ways, go your ways. I knew what you would prove; my friends told me as much, and I thought no less. That flattering tongue of yours won 165 me. 'Tis but one cast away, and so, come death! Two o'clock is your hour?

Orlando

Ay, sweet Rosalind.

Rosalind

By my troth, and in good earnest, and so God mend me, and by all pretty oaths that are not dangerous, if 170 you break one jot of your promise, or come one minute behind your hour, I will think you the most pathetical break-promise, and the most hollow lover, and the most unworthy of her you call Rosalind, that may be chosen out of the gross band of the unfaithful. Therefore beware my censure, and keep your promise. 175

Orlando

With no less religion than if thou wert indeed my Rosalind; so, adieu.

Rosalind

Well, Time is the old justice that examines all such offenders, and let Time try.

Adieu. *[Exit* ORLANDO.*]* 180

Celia

You have simply misus'd our sex in your love-prate. We must have your doublet and hose pluck'd over your head, and show the world what the bird hath done to her own nest.

Rosalind

O coz, coz, coz, my pretty little coz, that thou didst 185 know how many fathom deep I am in love! But it cannot be sounded; my affection hath an unknown bottom, like the Bay of Portugal.

Celia

Or rather, bottomless; that as fast as you pour affection in, it runs out. 190

Rosalind

No; that same wicked bastard of Venus, that was begot of thought, conceiv'd of spleen, and born of madness; that blind rascally boy, that abuses every one's eyes because his own are out – let him be judge how deep I am in love. I'll tell thee, Aliena, I cannot be out of 195 the sight of Orlando. I'll go find a shadow, and sigh till he come.

Celia

And I'll sleep.

[Exeunt.]

Scene II

The forest.

[Enter JAQUES *and* LORDS, *in the habit of foresters.]*

Jaques
Which is he that killed the deer?
Lord
Sir, it was I.
Jaques
Let's present him to the Duke, like a Roman conqueror;
and it would do well to set the deer's horns upon his
5   head for a branch of victory. Have you no song, forester,
for this purpose?
Lord
Yes, sir.
Jaques
Sing it; 'tis no matter how it be in tune, so it make
noise enough.

[Song.]

10   What shall he have that kill'd the deer?
His leather skin and horns to wear.

[The rest shall bear this burden:]

Then sing him home.

Take thou no scorn to wear the horn;
It was a crest ere thou wast born.

15   Thy father's father wore it;
And thy father bore it.
The horn, the horn, the lusty horn,
Is not a thing to laugh to scorn.

[Exeunt.]

Scene III

The forest.

[Enter ROSALIND *and* CELIA.*]*

Rosalind

How say you now? Is it not past two o'clock? And here
much Orlando!

Celia

I warrant you, with pure love and troubled brain, he
hath ta'en his bow and arrows, and is gone forth – to
sleep. Look, who comes here.   5

[Enter SILVIUS*]*

Silvius

My errand is to you, fair youth;
My gentle Phebe did bid me give you this.
I know not the contents; but, as I guess
By the stern brow and waspish action
Which she did use as she was writing of it,   10
It bears an angry tenour. Pardon me,
I am but as a guiltless messenger.

Rosalind

Patience herself would startle at this letter,
And play the swaggerer. Bear this, bear all.
She says I am not fair, that I lack manners;   15
She calls me proud, and that she could not love me,
Were man as rare as Phoenix. 'Od's my will!
Her love is not the hare that I do hunt;
Why writes she so to me? Well, shepherd, well,
This is a letter of your own device.   20

Silvius

No, I protest, I know not the contents; Phebe did
write it.

Rosalind

                    Come, come, you are a fool,
And turn'd into the extremity of love.

I saw her hand; she has a leathern hand,
25   A freestone-colour'd hand; I verily did think
That her old gloves were on, but 'twas her hands;
She has a huswife's hand – but that's no matter.
I say she never did invent this letter:
This is a man's invention, and his hand.

Silvius

30   Sure, it is hers.

Rosalind

Why, 'tis a boisterous and a cruel style;
A style for challengers. Why, she defies me,
Like Turk to Christian. Women's gentle brain
Could not drop forth such giant-rude invention,
35   Such Ethiope words, blacker in their effect
Than in their countenance. Will you hear the letter?

Silvius

So please you, for I never heard it yet;
Yet heard too much of Phebe's cruelty.

Rosalind

She Phebes me: mark how the tyrant writes. *[Reads.]*

40   'Art thou god to shepherd turn'd
        That a maiden's heart hath burn'd?'

Can a woman rail thus?

Silvius

Call you this railing?

Rosalind

        'Why, thy godhead laid apart,
45   War'st thou with a woman's heart?'

Did you ever hear such railing?

        'Whiles the eye of man did woo me,
        That could do no vengeance to me.'

Meaning me a beast.

50   'If the scorn of your bright eyne
        Have power to raise such love in mine,

Alack, in me what strange effect
Would they work in mild aspect!
Whiles you chid me, I did love;
How then might your prayers move!   55
He that brings this love to thee
Little knows this love in me;
And by him seal up thy mind,
Whether that thy youth and kind
Will the faithful offer take   60
Of me and all that I can make;
Or else by him my love deny,
And then I'll study how to die.'

Silvius

Call you this chiding?

Celia

Alas, poor shepherd!   65

Rosalind

Do you pity him? No, he deserves no pity. Wilt thou
love such a woman? What, to make thee an instrument,
and play false strains upon thee! Not to be endur'd!
Well, go your way to her, for I see love hath made
thee a tame snake, and say this to her – that if she 70
love me, I charge her to love thee; if she will not, I
will never have her unless thou entreat for her. If you
be a true lover, hence, and not a word; for here comes
more company. *[Exit* SILVIUS.*]*

[Enter OLIVER.*]*

Oliver

Good morrow, fair ones; pray you, if you know,   75
Where in the purlieus of this forest stands
A sheep-cote fenc'd about with olive trees?

Celia

West of this place, down in the neighbour bottom.
The rank of osiers by the murmuring stream
Left on your right hand brings you to the place.   80
But at this hour the house doth keep itself;

There's none within.

Oliver

If that an eye may profit by a tongue,
Then should I know you by description –
85   Such garments, and such years: 'The boy is fair,
Of female favour, and bestows himself
Like a ripe sister; the woman low,
And browner than her brother'. Are not you
The owner of the house I did inquire for?

Celia

90   It is no boast, being ask'd, to say we are.

Oliver

Orlando doth commend him to you both;
And to that youth he calls his Rosalind
He sends this bloody napkin. Are you he?

Rosalind

I am. What must we understand by this?

Oliver

95   Some of my shame; if you will know of me
What man I am, and how, and why, and where,
This handkercher was stain'd.

Celia

                                   I pray you, tell it.

Oliver

When last the young Orlando parted from you,
He left a promise to return again
100 Within an hour; and, pacing through the forest,
Chewing the food of sweet and bitter fancy,
Lo, what befell! He threw his eye aside,
And mark what object did present itself.
Under an oak, whose boughs were moss'd with age,
105 And high top bald with dry antiquity,
A wretched ragged man, o'ergrown with hair,
Lay sleeping on his back. About his neck
A green and gilded snake had wreath'd itself,
Who with her head nimble in threats approach'd
110 The opening of his mouth; but suddenly,

Seeing Orlando, it unlink'd itself,
And with indented glides did slip away
Into a bush; under which bush's shade
A lioness, with udders all drawn dry,
Lay couching, head on ground, with catlike watch,   115
When that the sleeping man should stir; for 'tis
The royal disposition of that beast
To prey on nothing that doth seem as dead.
This seen, Orlando did approach the man,
And found it was his brother, his elder brother.   120

Celia

O, I have heard him speak of that same brother;
And he did render him the most unnatural
That liv'd amongst men.

Oliver

               And well he might so do,
For well I know he was unnatural.

Rosalind

But, to Orlando: did he leave him there,   125
Food to the suck'd and hungry lioness?

Oliver

Twice did he turn his back, and purpos'd so;
But kindness, nobler ever than revenge,
And nature, stronger than his just occasion
Made him give battle to the lioness,   130
Who quickly fell before him; in which hurtling
From miserable slumber I awak'd.

Celia

Are you his brother?

Rosalind

             Was't you he rescu'd?

Celia

Was't you that did so oft contrive to kill him?

Oliver

'Twas I; but 'tis not I. I do not shame   135
To tell you what I was, since my conversion
So sweetly tastes, being the thing I am.

Rosalind
But for the bloody napkin?
Oliver

By and by.
When from the first to last, betwixt us two,
140   Tears our recountments had most kindly bath'd,
As how I came into that desert place –
In brief, he led me to the gentle Duke,
Who gave me fresh array and entertainment,
Committing me unto my brother's love;
145   Who led me instantly unto his cave,
There stripp'd himself, and here upon his arm
The lioness had torn some flesh away,
Which all this while had bled; and now he fainted,
And cried, in fainting, upon Rosalind.
150   Brief, I recover'd him, bound up his wound,
And, after some small space, being strong at heart,
He sent me hither, stranger as I am,
To tell this story, that you might excuse
His broken promise, and to give this napkin,
155   Dy'd in his blood, unto the shepherd youth
That he in sport doth call his Rosalind.

[ROSALIND swoons.]

Celia
Why, how now, Ganymede! sweet Ganymede!
Oliver
Many will swoon when they do look on blood.
Celia
There is more in it. Cousin Ganymede!
Oliver
160   Look, he recovers.
Rosalind
I would I were at home.
Celia

We'll lead you thither.
I pray you, will you take him by the arm?

Oliver

Be of good cheer, youth. You a man!
You lack a man's heart.

Rosalind

I do so, I confess it. Ah, sirrah, a body would think 165
this was well counterfeited. I pray you tell your brother
how well I counterfeited. Heigh-ho!

Oliver

This was not counterfeit; there is too great testimony
in your complexion that it was a passion of earnest.

Rosalind

Counterfeit, I assure you. 170

Oliver

Well then, take a good heart and counterfeit to be a
man.

Rosalind

So I do; but, i' faith, I should have been a woman by
right.

Celia

Come, you look paler and paler; pray you draw home- 175
wards. Good sir, go with us.

Oliver

That will I, for I must bear answer back
How you excuse my brother, Rosalind.

Rosalind

I shall devise something; but, I pray you, commend
my counterfeiting to him. Will you go? 180

[Exeunt.]

ACT FIVE
Scene I

The forest.

[Enter TOUCHSTONE *and* AUDREY.*]*

Touchstone
We shall find a time, Audrey; patience, gentle Audrey.
Audrey
Faith, the priest was good enough, for all the old gentleman's saying.
Touchstone
A most wicked Sir Oliver, Audrey, a most vile Martext.
5   But, Audrey, there is a youth here in the forest lays claim to you.
Audrey
Ay, I know who 'tis; he hath no interest in me in the world; here comes the man you mean.

[Enter WILLIAM.*]*

Touchstone
It is meat and drink to me to see a clown. By my troth,
10   we that have good wits have good wits have much to answer for: we shall be flouting; we cannot hold.
William
Good ev'n, Audrey.
Audrey
God ye good ev'n, William.
William
And good ev'n, to you, sir.
Touchstone
15   Good ev'n, gentle friend. Cover thy head, cover thy head; nay, prithee be cover'd. How old are you, friend?
William
Five and twenty, sir.

Touchstone

A ripe age. Is thy name William?

William

William, sir.

Touchstone

A fair name. Wast born i' th' forest here?   20

William

Ay, sir, I thank God.

Touchstone

'Thank God.' A good answer. Art rich?

William

Faith, sir, so so.

Touchstone

'So so' is good, very good, very excellent good; and
yet it is not; it is but so so.   25
Art thou wise?

William

Ay, sir, I have a pretty wit.

Touchstone

Why, thou say'st well. I do now remember a saying:
'The fool doth think he is wise, but the wise man
knows himself to be a fool'. The heathen philosopher, 30
when he had a desire to eat a grape, would open his
lips when he put it into his mouth; meaning thereby
that grapes were made to eat and lips to open. You do
love this maid?

William

I do, sir.   35

Touchstone

Give me your hand. Art thou learned?

William

No, sir.

Touchstone

Then learn this of me: to have is to have; for it is a
figure in rhetoric that drink, being pour'd out of a cup
into a glass, by filling the one doth empty the other; 40

for all your writers do consent that ipse is he; now, you
are not ipse, for I am he.

William

Which he, sir?

Touchstone

He, sir, that must marry this woman. Therefore, you
45   clown, abandon – which is in the vulgar leave – the
society – which in the boorish is company – of this
female – which in the common is woman – which
together is: abandon the society of this female; or,
clown, thou perishest; or, to thy better understanding,
50   diest; or, to wit, I kill thee, make thee away, translate
thy life into death, thy liberty into bondage. I will deal
in poison with thee, or in bastinado, or in steel; I will
bandy with thee in faction; I will o'er-run thee with
policy; I will kill thee a hundred and fifty ways; there-
55   fore tremble, and depart.

Audrey

Do, good William.

William

God rest you merry, sir. *[Exit.]*

[Enter CORIN.*]*

Corin

Our master and mistress seeks you; come away, away.

Touchstone

Trip, Audrey, trip, Audrey. I attend, I attend.

[Exeunt.]

Scene II

The forest.

[Enter ORLANDO *and* OLIVER.*]*

Orlando
   Is't possible that on so little acquaintance you should
   like her? that but seeing you should love her? and
   loving woo? and, wooing, she should grant? and will
   you persever to enjoy her?
Oliver
   Neither call the giddiness of it in question, the poverty   5
   of her, the small acquaintance, my sudden wooing,
   nor her sudden consenting; but say with me, I love
   Aliena; say with her that she loves me; consent with
   both that we may enjoy each other. It shall be to your
   good; for my father's house and all the revenue that   10
   was old Sir Rowland's will I estate upon you, and here
   live and die a shepherd.
Orlando
   You have my consent. Let your wedding be to-morrow.
   Thither will I invite the Duke and all's contented
   followers. Go you and prepare Aliena; for, look you,   15
   here comes my Rosalind.

[Enter ROSALIND.*]*

Rosalind
   God save you, brother.
Oliver
   And you, fair sister. *[Exit.]*
Rosalind
   O, my dear Orlando, how it grieves me to see thee
   wear thy heart in a scarf!   20
Orlando
   It is my arm.
Rosalind
   I thought thy heart had been wounded with the claws
   of a lion.

Orlando
Wounded it is, but with the eyes of a lady.
Rosalind
25 Did your brother tell you how I counterfeited to swoon
when he show'd me your handkercher.
Orlando
Ay, and greater wonders than that.
Rosalind
O, I know where you are. Nay, 'tis true. There was
never any thing so sudden but the fight of two rams
30 and Caesar's thrasonical brag of 'I came, saw, and
overcame'. For your brother and my sister no sooner
met but they look'd; no sooner look'd but they lov'd;
no sooner lov'd but they sigh'd; no sooner sigh'd but
they ask'd one another the reason; no sooner knew
35 the reason but they sought the remedy – and in these
degrees have they made a pair of stairs to marriage,
which they will climb incontinent, or else be incontinent before marriage. They are in the very wrath of
love, and they will together. Clubs cannot part them.
Orlando
40 They shall be married to-morrow; and I will bid the
Duke to the nuptial. But, O, how bitter a thing it is
to look into happiness through another man's eyes!
By so much the more shall I to-morrow be at the height
of heart-heaviness, by how much I shall think my
45 brother happy in having what he wishes for.
Rosalind
Why, then, to-morrow I cannot serve your turn for
Rosalind?
Orlando
I can live no longer by thinking.
Rosalind
I will weary you, then, no longer with idle talking.
50 Know of me then – for now I speak to some purpose
– that I know you are a gentleman of good conceit. I
speak not this that you should bear a good opinion of

my knowledge, insomuch I say I know you are; neither
do I labour for a greater esteem than may in some
little measure draw a belief from you, to do yourself 55
good, and not to grace me. Believe then, if you please,
that I can do strange things. I have, since I was three
year old, convers'd with a magician, most profound in
his art and yet not damnable. If you do love Rosalind
so near the heart as your gesture cries it out, when 60
your brother marries Aliena shall you marry her. I
know into what straits of fortune she is driven; and it
is not impossible to me, if it appear not inconvenient
to you, to set her before your eyes to-morrow, human
as she is, and without any danger. 65

Orlando

Speak'st thou in sober meanings?

Rosalind

By my life, I do; which I tender dearly, though I say
I am a magician. Therefore put you in your best array,
bid your friends; for if you will be married to-morrow,
you shall; and to Rosalind, if you will. 70

[Enter SILVIUS and PHEBE.]

Look, here comes a lover of mine, and a lover of hers.

Phebe

Youth, you have done me much ungentleness
To show the letter that I writ to you.

Rosalind

I care not if I have. It is my study
To seem despiteful and ungentle to you. 75
You are there follow'd by a faithful shepherd;
Look upon him, love him, he worships you.

Phebe

Good shepherd, tell this youth what 'tis to love.

Silvius

It is to be all made of sighs and tears;
And so am I for Phebe. 80

Phebe
And I for Ganymede.

Orlando
And I for Rosalind.

Rosalind
And I for no woman.

Silvius
It is to be all made of faith and service;
85   And so am I for Phebe.

Phebe
And I for Ganymede.

Orlando
And I for Rosalind.

Rosalind
And I for no woman.

Silvius
It is to be all made of fantasy,
90   All made of passion, and all made of wishes;
All adoration, duty, and observance,
All humbleness, all patience, and impatience,
All purity, all trial, all obedience;
And so am I for Phebe.

Phebe
95   And so am I for Ganymede.

Orlando
And so am I for Rosalind.

Rosalind
And so am I for no woman.

Phebe
If this be so, why blame you me to love you?

Silvius
If this be so, why blame you me to love you?

Orlando
100   If this be so, why blame you me to love you?

Rosalind
Why do you speak too 'why blame you me to love
you?'

Orlando

To her that is not here, nor doth not hear.

Rosalind

Pray you, no more of this; 'tis like the howling of irish
wolves against the moon. *[To* SILVIUS*]* I will help you 105
if I can. *[To* PHEBE*]* I would love you if I could. –
To-morrow meet me all together. *[To* PHEBE*]* I will marry
you if ever I marry woman, and I'll be married
tomorrow. *[To* ORLANDO*]* I will satisfy you if ever I
satisfied man, and you shall be married tomorrow. *[To* 110
SILVIUS*]* I will content you if what pleases you contents
you, and you shall be married to-morrow. *[To* ORLANDO*]*
as you love Rosalind, meet. *[To* SILVIUS*]* as you love
Phebe, meet; – and as I love no woman, I'll meet. So,
fare you well; I have left you commands. 115

Silvius

I'll not fail, if I live.

Phebe

Nor I.

Orlando

Nor I.

[Exeunt.]

Scene III

The forest.

[Enter TOUCHSTONE *and* AUDREY.]*

Touchstone
  To-morrow is the joyful day,
  Audrey; to-morrow will we be married.
Audrey
  I do desire it with all my heart; and I hope it is no
  dishonest desire to desire to be a woman of the world.
5 Here come two of the banish'd Duke's pages.

[Enter two Pages.]

1 Page
  Well met, honest gentlemen.
Touchstone
  By my troth, well met. Come sit, sit, and a song.
2 Page
  We are for you; sit i' th' middle.
1 Page
  Shall we clap into't roundly, without hawking, or spit-
10 ting, or saying we are hoarse, which are the only
  prologues to a bad voice?
2 Page
  I'faith; i'faith; and both in a tune, like two gipsies on
  a horse.

[Song.]

  It was a lover and his lass,
15   With a hey, and a ho, and a hey nonino,
  That o'er the green corn-field did pass
    In the spring time, the only pretty ring time,
  When birds do sing, hey ding a ding, ding.
    Sweet lovers love the spring.
20 Between the acres of the rye,
    With a hey, and a ho, and a hey nonino,

These pretty country folks would lie,
    In the spring time, etc.
This carol they began that hour,
    With a hey, and a ho, and a hey nonino,   25
How that a life was but a flower,
    In the spring time, etc.
And therefore take the present time,
    With a hey, and a ho, and a hey nonino,
For love is crowned with the prime,   30
    In the spring time, etc.

Touchstone

Truly, young gentlemen, though there was no great matter in the ditty, yet the note was very untuneable.

1 Page

You are deceiv'd, sir; we kept time, we lost not our 35 time.

Touchstone

By my troth, yes; I count it but time lost to hear such a foolish song. God buy you; and God mend your voices. Come, Audrey.

[Exeunt.]

Scene IV

The forest.

[*Enter* DUKE SENIOR, AMIENS, JAQUES, ORLANDO,
OLIVER, *and* CELIA.]

Duke Senior
    Dost thou believe, Orlando, that the boy
    Can do all this that he hath promised?
Orlando
    I sometimes do believe and sometimes do not;
    As those that fear they hope, and know they fear.

[*Enter* ROSALIND, SILVIUS, *and* PHEBE.]

Rosalind
5   Patience once more, whiles our compact is urg'd:
    You say, if I bring in your Rosalind,
    You will bestow her on Orlando here?
Duke Senior
    That would I, had I kingdoms to give with her.
Rosalind
    And you say you will have her when I bring her?
Orlando
10   That would I, were I of all kingdoms king.
Rosalind
    You say you'll marry me, if I be willing?
Phebe
    That will I, should I die the hour after.
Rosalind
    But if you do refuse to marry me,
    You'll give yourself to this most faithful shepherd?
Phebe
15   So is the bargain.
Rosalind
    You say that you'll have Phebe, if she will?
Silvius
    Though to have her and death were both one thing.

Rosalind
I have promis'd to make all this matter even.
Keep you your word, O Duke, to give your daughter;
You yours, Orlando, to receive his daughter; 20
Keep your word, Phebe, that you'll marry me,
Or else, refusing me, to wed this shepherd;
Keep your word, Silvius, that you'll marry her
If she refuse me; and from hence I go,
To make these doubts all even. 25

[Exeunt ROSALIND *and* CELIA.*]*

Duke Senior
I do remember in this shepherd boy
Some lively touches of my daughter's favour.
Orlando
My lord, the first time that I ever saw him
Methought he was a brother to your daughter.
But, my good lord, this boy is forest-born, 30
And hath been tutor'd in the rudiments
Of many desperate studies by his uncle,
Whom he reports to be a great magician,
Obscured in the circle of this forest.

[Enter TOUCHSTONE *and* AUDREY.*]*

Jaques
There is, sure, another flood toward, and these couples 35
are coming to the ark. Here comes a pair of very strange
beasts which in all tongues are call'd fools.
Touchstone
Salutation and greeting to you all!
Jaques
Good my lord, bid him welcome. This is the motley-
minded gentleman that I have so often met in the 40
forest. He hath been a courtier, he swears.
Touchstone
If any man doubt that, let him put me to my purga-
tion. I have trod a measure; I have flatt'red a lady; I

45 have been politic with my friend, smooth with mine
enemy; I have undone three tailors; I have had four
quarrels, and like to have fought one.

Jaques

And how was that ta'en up?

Touchstone

Faith, we met, and found the quarrel was upon the
seventh cause.

Jaques

50 How seventh cause? Good my lord, like this fellow.

Duke Senior

I like him very well.

Touchstone

God 'ild you, sir; I desire you of the like. I press in
here, sir, amongst the rest of the country copulatives,
to swear and to forswear, according as marriage binds

55 and blood breaks. A poor virgin, sir, an ill-favour'd
thing, sir, but mine own; a poor humour of mine, sir,
to take that that no man else will. Rich honesty dwells
like a miser, sir, in a poor house; as your pearl in your
foul oyster.

Duke Senior

60 By my faith, he is very swift and sententious.

Touchstone

According to the fool's bolt, sir, and such dulcet
diseases.

Jaques

But, for the seventh cause: how did you find the quarrel
on the seventh cause?

Touchstone

65 Upon a lie seven times removed – bear your body more
seeming, Audrey – as thus, sir. I did dislike the cut of
a certain courtier's beard; he sent me word, if I said
his beard was not cut well, he was in the mind it was.
This is call'd the Retort Courteous. If I sent him word

70 again it was not well cut, he would send me word he
cut it to please himself. This is call'd the Quip Modest.

If again it was not well cut, he disabled my judgment.
This is call'd the Reply Churlish. If again it was not
well cut, he would answer I spake not true. This is
call'd the Reproof Valiant. If again it was not well cut, 75
he would say I lie. This is call'd the Countercheck
Quarrelsome. And so to Lie Circumstantial and the Lie
Direct.

Jaques

And how oft did you say his beard was not well cut?

Touchstone

I durst go no further than the Lie Circumstantial, nor 80
he durst not give me the Lie Direct; and so we measur'd
swords and parted.

Jaques

Can you nominate in order now the degrees of the
lie?

Touchstone

O, sir, we quarrel in print by the book, as you have 85
books for good manners. I will name you the degrees.
The first, the Retort Courteous; the second, the Quip
Modest; the third, the Reply Churlish; the fourth, the
Reproof Valiant; the fifth, the Countercheck
Quarrelsome; the sixth, the Lie with Circumstance; the 90
seventh, the Lie Direct. All these you may avoid but
the Lie Direct; and you may avoid that too with an If.
I knew when seven justices could not take up a quarrel;
but when the parties were met themselves, one of them
thought but of an If, as: 'If you said so, then I said so'. 95
And they shook hands, and swore brothers. Your If is
the only peace-maker; much virtue in If.

Jaques

Is not this a rare fellow, my lord? He's as good at any
thing, and yet a fool.

Duke Senior

He uses his folly like a stalkinghorse, and under the 100
presentation of that he shoots his wit.

[Enter HYMEN, ROSALIND, and CELIA. Still music.]

Hymen
>Then is there mirth in heaven,
>When earthly things made even
>>Atone together.
105 Good Duke, receive thy daughter;
>Hymen from heaven brought her,
>>Yea, brought her hither,
>That thou mightst join her hand with
>>his,
>Whose heart within his bosom is.

Rosalind
110 [To DUKE] To you I give myself, for I am yours.
[To ORLANDO] To you I give myself, for I am yours.
Duke Senior
If there be truth in sight, you are my daughter.
Orlando
If there be truth in sight, you are my Rosalind.
Phebe
If sight and shape be true,
115 Why then, my love adieu!
Rosalind
I'll have no father, if you be not he;
I'll have no husband, if you be not he;
Nor ne'er wed woman, if you be not she.
Hymen
>Peace, ho! I bar confusion;
120 'Tis I must make conclusion
>>Of these most strange events.
>Here's eight that must take hands
>To join in Hymen's bands,
>>If truth holds true contents.
125 You and you no cross shall part;
>You and you are heart in heart;
>You to his love must accord,
>Or have a woman to your lord;
>You and you are sure together,
130 As the winter to foul weather.

> Whiles a wedlock-hymn we sing,
> Feed yourselves with questioning,
> That reason wonder may diminish,

How thus we met, and these things finish.

[Song.]

Wedding is great Juno's crown;   135
   O blessed bond of board and bed!
'Tis Hymen peoples every town;
   High wedlock then be honoured.
Honour, high honour, and renown,
To Hymen, god of every town!   140

Duke Senior
   O my dear niece, welcome thou art to me!
   Even daughter, welcome in no less degree.
Phebe
   I will not eat my word, now thou art mine;
   Thy faith my fancy to thee doth combine.

[Enter JAQUES DE BOYS.*]*

Jaques De Boys
   Let me have audience for a word or two.   145
   I am the second son of old Sir Rowland,
   That bring these tidings to this fair assembly.
   Duke Frederick, hearing how that every day
   Men of great worth resorted to this forest,
   Address'd a mighty power; which were on foot,   150
   In his own conduct, purposely to take
   His brother here, and put him to the sword;
   And to the skirts of this wild wood he came,
   Where, meeting with an old religious man,
   After some question with him, was converted   155
   Both from his enterprise and from the world;
   His crown bequeathing to his banish'd brother,
   And all their lands restor'd to them again
   That were with him exil'd. This to be true

I do engage my life.
Duke Senior
160   Welcome, young man.
Thou offer'st fairly to thy brothers' wedding:
To one, his lands withheld; and to the other,
A land itself at large, a potent dukedom.
First, in this forest let us do those ends
165 That here were well begun and well begot;
And after, every of this happy number,
That have endur'd shrewd days and nights with us,
Shall share the good of our returned fortune,
According to the measure of their states.
170 Meantime, forget this new-fall'n dignity,
And fall into our rustic revelry.
Play, music; and you brides and bridegrooms all,
With measure heap'd in joy, to th' measures fall.
Jaques
Sir, by your patience. If I heard you rightly,
175 The Duke hath put on a religious life,
And thrown into neglect the pompous court.
Jaques De Boys
He hath.
Jaques
To him will I. Out of these convertites
There is much matter to be heard and learn'd
180 *[To* DUKE*]* You to your former honour I bequeath;
Your patience and your virtue well deserves it.
[To ORLANDO.*]* You to a love that your true faith
     doth merit;
[To OLIVER*]* You to your land, and love, and great
     allies;
[To SILVIUS*]* You to a long and well-deserved bed;
[To TOUCHSTONE*]* And you to wrangling; for thy
185   loving voyage
Is but for two months victuall'd. – So to your
     pleasures;
I am for other than for dancing measures.

Duke Senior
Stay, Jaques, stay.
Jaques
To see no pastime I. What you would have
I'll stay to know at your abandon'd cave. *[Exit.]*   190
Duke Senior
Proceed, proceed. We will begin these rites,
As we do trust they'll end, in true delights.

[A dance. Exeunt.]

EPILOGUE

Rosalind

It is not the fashion to see the lady the epilogue; but it is no more unhandsome than to see the lord the prologue. If it be true that good wine needs no bush, 'tis true that a good play needs no epilogue. Yet to good wine they do use good bushes; and good plays prove the better by the help of good epilogues. What a case am I in then, that am neither a good epilogue, nor cannot insinuate with you in the behalf of a good play! I am not furnish'd like a beggar; therefore to beg will not become me. My way is to conjure you; and I'll begin with the women. I charge you, O women, for the love you bear to men, to like as much of this play as please you; and I charge you, O men, for the love you bear to women – as I perceive by your simp'ring none of you hates them – that between you and the women the play may please. If I were a woman, I would kiss as many of you as had beards that pleas'd me, complexions that lik'd me, and breaths that I defied not; and, I am sure, as many as have good beards, or good faces, or sweet breaths, will, for my kind offer, when I make curtsy, bid me farewell.

Shakespeare:
Words and Phrases

adapted from the Collins English Dictionary

abate 1 VERB to abate here means to lessen or diminish ❑ *There lives within the very flame of love/A kind of wick or snuff that will abate it* (Hamlet 4.7) 2 VERB to abate here means to shorten ❑ *Abate thy hours* (A Midsummer Night's Dream 3.2) 3 VERB to abate here means to deprive ❑ *She hath abated me of half my train* (King Lear 2.4)

abjure VERB to abjure means to renounce or give up ❑ *this rough magic I here abjure* (Tempest 5.1)

abroad ADV abroad means elsewhere or everywhere ❑ *You have heard of the news abroad* (King Lear 2.1)

abrogate VERB to abrogate means to put an end to ❑ *so it shall praise you to abrogate scurrility* (Love's Labours Lost 4.2)

abuse 1 NOUN abuse in this context means deception or fraud ❑ *What should this mean? Are all the rest come back?/Or is it some abuse, and no such thing?* (Hamlet 4.7) 2 NOUN an abuse in this context means insult or offence ❑ *I will be deaf to pleading and excuses/Nor tears nor prayers shall purchase our abuses* (Romeo and Juliet 3.1) 3 NOUN an abuse in this context means using something improperly ❑ *we'll digest/Th'abuse*

of distance (Henry II Chorus) 4 NOUN an abuse in this context means doing something which is corrupt or dishonest ❑ *Come, bring them away: if these be good people in a commonweal that do nothing but their abuses in common houses, I know no law: bring them away.* (Measure for Measure 2.1)

abuser NOUN the abuser here is someone who betrays, a betrayer ❑ *I ... do attach thee/For an abuser of the world* (Othello 1.2)

accent NOUN accent here means language ❑ *In states unborn, and accents yet unknown* (Julius Caesar 3.1)

accident NOUN an accident in this context is an event or something that happened ❑ *think no more of this night's accidents* (A Midsummer Night's Dream 4.1)

accommodate VERB to accommodate in this context means to equip or to give someone the equipment to do something ❑ *The safer sense will ne'er accommodate/His master thus.* (King Lear 4.6)

according ADJ according means sympathetic or ready to agree ❑ *within the scope of choice/Lies* my consent and fair according voice (*Romeo and Juliet 1.2*)

account NOUN account often means judgement (by God) or reckoning ❑ *No reckoning made, but sent to my account/With all my imperfections on my head* (*Hamlet 1.5*)

accountant ADJ accountant here means answerable or accountable ❑ *his offence is… /Accountant to the law* (*Measure for Measure 2.4*)

ace NOUN ace here means one or first referring to the lowest score on a dice ❑ *No die, but an ace, for him; for he is but one./Less than an ace, man; for he is dead; he is nothing.* (*A Midsummer Night's Dream 5.1*)

acquit VERB here acquit means to be rid of or free of. It is related to the verb quit ❑ *I am glad I am so acquit of this tinderbox* (*The Merry Wives of Windsor 1.3*)

afeard ADJ afeard means afraid or frightened ❑ *Nothing afeard of what thyself didst make* (*Macbeth 1.3*)

affiance NOUN affiance means confidence or trust ❑ *O how hast thou with jealousy infected/The sweetness of affiance* (*Henry V 2.2*)

affinity NOUN in this context, affinity means important connections, or relationships with important people ❑ *The Moor replies/That he you hurt is of great fame in Cyprus,/And great affinity* (*Othello 3.1*)

agnize VERB to agnize is an old word that means that you recognize or acknowledge something ❑ *I do agnize/A natural and prompt alacrity I find in hardness* (*Othello 1.3*)

ague NOUN an ague is a fever in which the patient has hot and cold

shivers one after the other ❑ *This is some monster of the isle with four legs, who hath got … an ague* (*The Tempest 2.2*)

alarm, alarum NOUN an alarm or alarum is a call to arms or a signal for soldiers to prepare to fight ❑ *Whence cometh this alarum and the noise?* (*Henry VI part I 1.4*)

Albion NOUN Albion is another word for England ❑ *but I will sell my dukedom,/ To buy a slobbery and a dirty farm In that nook-shotten isle of Albion* (*Henry V 3.5*)

all of all PHRASE all of all means everything, or the sum of all things ❑ *The very all of all* (*Love's Labours Lost 5.1*)

amend VERB amend in this context means to get better or to heal ❑ *at his touch… They presently amend* (*Macbeth 4.3*)

anchor VERB if you anchor on something you concentrate on it or fix on it ❑ *My invention … Anchors on Isabel* (*Measure for Measure 2.4*)

anon ADV anon was a common word for soon ❑ *You shall see anon how the murderer gets the love of Gonzago's wife* (*Hamlet 3.2*)

antic 1 ADJ antic here means weird or strange ❑ *I'll charm the air to give a sound/While you perform your antic round* (*Macbeth 4.1*) 2 NOUN in this context antic means a clown or a strange, unattractive creature ❑ *If black, why nature, drawing an antic,/ Made a foul blot* (*Much Ado About Nothing 3.1*)

apace ADV apace was a common word for quickly ❑ *Come apace* (*As You Like It 3.3*)

apparel NOUN apparel means clothes or clothing ❑ *one suit of apparel* (*Hamlet 3.2*)

appliance NOUN appliance here means cure ❑ *Diseases desperate grown/By desperate appliance are relieved* (*Hamlet 4.3*)

argument NOUN argument here means a topic of conversation or the subject ❑ *Why 'tis the rarest argument of wonder that hath shot out in our latter times* (*All's Well That Ends Well 2.3*)

arrant ADJ arrant means absolute, complete. It strengthens the meaning of a noun ❑ *Fortune, that arrant whore* (*King Lear 2.4*)

arras NOUN an arras is a tapestry, a large cloth with a picture sewn on it using coloured thread ❑ *Behind the arras I'll convey myself/To hear the process* (*Hamlet 3.3*)

art 1 NOUN art in this context means knowledge ❑ *Their malady convinces/The great essay of art* (*Macbeth 4.3*) 2 NOUN art can also mean skill as it does here ❑ *He ... gave you such a masterly report/For art and exercise in your defence* (*Hamlet 4.7*) 3 NOUN art here means magic ❑ *Now I want/Spirits to enforce, art to enchant* (*The Tempest 5 Epilogue*)

assay 1 NOUN an assay was an attempt, a try ❑ *Make assay./Bow, stubborn knees* (*Hamlet 3.3*) 2 NOUN assay can also mean a test or a trial ❑ *he hath made assay of her virtue* (*Measure for Measure 3.1*)

attend (on/upon) VERB attend on means to wait for or to expect ❑ *Tarry I here, I but attend on death* (*Two Gentlemen of Verona 3.1*)

auditor NOUN an auditor was a member of an audience or someone who listens ❑ *I'll be an auditor* (*A Midsummer Night's Dream 3.1*)

aught NOUN aught was a common word which meant anything ❑ *if my love thou holdest at aught* (*Hamlet 4.3*)

aunt 1 NOUN an aunt was another word for an old woman and also means someone who talks a lot or a gossip ❑ *The wisest aunt telling the saddest tale* (*A Midsummer Night's Dream 2.1*) 2 NOUN aunt could also mean a mistress or a prostitute ❑ *the thrush and the jay/Are summer songs for me and my aunts/While we lie tumbling in the hay* (*The Winter's Tale 4.3*)

avaunt EXCLAM avaunt was a common word which meant go away ❑ *Avaunt, you curs!* (*King Lear 3.6*)

aye ADV here aye means always or ever ❑ *Whose state and honour I for aye allow* (*Richard II 5.2*)

baffle VERB baffle meant to be disgraced in public or humiliated ❑ *I am disgraced, impeached, and baffled here* (*Richard II 1.1*)

bald ADJ bald means trivial or silly ❑ *I knew 'twould be a bald conclusion* (*The Comedy of Errors 2.2*)

ban NOUN a ban was a curse or an evil spell ❑ *Sometimes with lunatic bans... Enforce their charity* (*King Lear 2.3*)

barren ADJ barren meant empty or hollow ❑ *now I let go your hand, I am barren.* (*Twelfth Night 1.3*)

base ADJ base is an adjective that means unworthy or dishonourable ❑ *civet is of a baser birth than tar* (*As You Like It 3.2*)

base 1 ADJ base can also mean of low social standing or someone who was not part of the ruling class ❑ *Why brand they us with 'base'?* (*King Lear 1.2*) 2 ADJ here base means poor quality ❑ *Base cousin,/ Darest thou break first?* (*Two Noble Kinsmen 3.3*)

bawdy NOUN bawdy means obscene or rude ❑ *Bloody, bawdy villain!* (*Hamlet 2.2*)

bear in hand PHRASE bear in hand means taken advantage of or fooled ❑ *This I made good to you In our last conference, passed in probation with you/ How you were borne in hand* (*Macbeth 3.1*)

beard VERB to beard someone was to oppose or confront them ❑ *Com'st thou to beard me in Denmark?* (*Hamlet 2.2*)

beard, in one's PHRASE if you say something in someone's beard you say it to their face ❑ *I will verify as much in his beard* (*Henry V 3.2*)

beaver NOUN a beaver was a visor on a battle helmet ❑ *O yes, my lord, he wore his beaver up* (*Hamlet 1.2*)

become VERB if something becomes you it suits you or is appropriate to you ❑ *Nothing in his life became him like the leaving it* (*Macbeth 1.4*)

bed, brought to PHRASE to be brought to bed means to give birth ❑ *His wife but yesternight was brought to bed* (*Titus Andronicus 4.2*)

bedabbled ADJ if something is bedabbled it is sprinkled ❑ *Bedabbled with the dew, and torn with briers* (*A Midsummer Night's Dream 3.2*)

Bedlam NOUN Bedlam was a word used for Bethlehem Hospital which was a place the insane were sent to ❑ *The country give me proof and precedent/ Of Bedlam beggars* (*King Lear 2.3*)

bed-swerver NOUN a bed-swerver was someone who was unfaithful in marriage, an adulterer ❑ *she's/A bed-swerver* (*Winter's Tale 2.1*)

befall 1 VERB to befall is to happen, occur or take place ❑ *In this same interlude it doth befall/That I present a wall* (*A Midsummer Night's Dream 5.1*) 2 VERB to befall can also mean to happen to someone or something ❑ *fair befall thee and thy noble house* (*Richard III 1.3*)

behoof NOUN behoof was an advantage or benefit ❑ *All our surgeons/ Convent in their behoof* (*Two Noble Kinsmen 1.4*)

beldam NOUN a beldam was a witch or old woman ❑ *Have I not reason, beldams as you are?* (*Macbeth 3.5*)

belike ADV belike meant probably, perhaps or presumably ❑ *belike he likes it not* (*Hamlet 3.2*)

bent 1 NOUN bent means a preference or a direction ❑ *Let me work,/ For I can give his humour true bent,/ And I will bring him to the Capitol* (*Julius Caesar 2.1*) 2 ADJ if you are bent on something you are determined to do it ❑ *for now I am bent to know/ By the worst means the worst.* (*Macbeth 3.4*)

beshrew VERB beshrew meant to curse or wish evil on someone ❑ *much beshrew my manners and my pride/ If Hermia meant to say Lysander lied* (*A Midsummer Night's Dream 2.2*)

betime (s) ADV betime means early
❏ *To business that we love we rise betime* (*Antony and Cleopatra 4.4*)

bevy NOUN bevy meant type or sort, it was also used to mean company ❏ *many more of the same bevy* (*Hamlet 5.2*)

blazon VERB to blazon something meant to display or show it ❏ *that thy skill be more to blazon it* (*Romeo and Juliet 2.6*)

blind ADJ if you are blind when you do something you are reckless or do not care about the consequences ❏ *are you yet to your own souls so blind/ That two you will war with God by murdering me* (*Richard III 1.4*)

bombast NOUN bombast was wool stuffing (used in a cushion for example) and so it came to mean padded out or long-winded. Here it means someone who talks a lot about nothing in particular ❏ *How now my sweet creature of bombast* (*Henry IV part I 2.4*)

bond 1 NOUN a bond is a contract or legal deed ❏ *Well, then, your bond, and let me see* (*Merchant of Venice 1.3*) 2 NOUN bond could also mean duty or commitment ❏ *I love your majesty/ According to my bond* (*King Lear 1.1*)

bottom NOUN here bottom means essence, main point or intent ❏ *Now I see/ The bottom of your purpose* (*All's Well That Ends Well 3.7*)

bounteously ADV bounteously means plentifully, abundantly ❏ *I prithee, and I'll pay thee bounteously* (*Twelfth Night 1.2*)

brace 1 NOUN a brace is a couple or two ❏ *Have lost a brace of kinsmen*

(*Romeo and Juliet 5.3*) 2 NOUN if you are in a brace position it means you are ready ❏ *For that it stands not in such warlike brace* (*Othello 1.3*)

brand VERB to mark permanently like the markings on cattle ❏ *the wheeled seat/ Of fortunate Caesar ... branded his baseness that ensued* (*Anthony and Cleopatra 4.14*)

brave ADJ brave meant fine, excellent or splendid ❏ *O brave new world/ That has such people in't* (*The Tempest 5.1*)

brine NOUN brine is sea-water ❏ *He shall drink nought brine, for I'll not show him/ Where the quick freshes are* (*The Tempest 3.2*)

brow NOUN brow in this context means appearance ❏ *doth hourly grow/ Out of his brows* (*Hamlet 3.3*)

burden 1 NOUN the burden here is a chorus ❏ *I would sing my song without a burden* (*As You Like It 3.2*) 2 NOUN burden means load or weight (this is the current meaning) ❏ *the scarfs and the bannerets about thee did manifoldly dissuade me from believing thee a vessel of too great a burden* (*All's Well that Ends Well 2.3*)

buttons, in one's PHRASE this is a phrase that means clear, easy to see ❏ *Tis in his buttons he will carry't* (*The Merry Wives of Windsor 3.2*)

cable NOUN cable here means scope or reach ❏ *The law ... Will give her cable* (*Othello 1.2*)

cadent ADJ if something is cadent it is falling or dropping ❏ *With cadent tears fret channels in her cheeks* (*King Lear 1.4*)

canker VERB to canker is to decay, become corrupt ❑ *And, as with age his body uglier grows,/ So his mind cankers* (*The Tempest 4.1*)

canon, from the PHRASE from the canon is an expression meaning out of order, improper ❑ *Twas from the canon* (*Coriolanus 3.1*)

cap-a-pie ADV cap-a-pie means from head to foot, completely ❑ *I am courtier cap-a-pie* (*The Winter's Tale 4.4*)

carbonadoed ADJ if something is carbonadoed it is cut or scored (scratched) with a knife ❑ *it is your carbonadoed* (*All's Well That Ends Well 4.5*)

carouse VERB to carouse is to drink at length, party ❑ *They cast their caps up and carouse together* (*Anthony and Cleopatra 4.12*)

carrack NOUN a carrack was a large old ship, a galleon ❑ *Faith, he tonight hath boarded a land-carrack* (*Othello 1.2*)

cassock NOUN a cassock here means a military cloak, long coat ❑ *half of the which dare not shake the snow from off their cassocks lest they shake themselves to pieces* (*All's Well That Ends Well 4.3*)

catastrophe NOUN catastrophe here means conclusion or end ❑ *pat he comes, like the catastrophe of the old comedy* (*King Lear 1.2*)

cautel NOUN a cautel was a trick or a deceptive act ❑ *Perhaps he loves you now/ And now no soil not cautel doth besmirch* (*Hamlet 1.2*)

celerity NOUN celerity was a common word for speed, swiftness ❑ *Hence hath offence his quick celerity/ When it is borne in high authority* (*Measure for Measure 4.2*)

chafe NOUN chafe meant anger or temper ❑ *this Herculean Roman does become/ The carriage of his chafe* (*Anthony and Cleopatra 1.3*)

chanson NOUN chanson was an old word for a song ❑ *The first row of the pious chanson will show you more* (*Hamlet 2.2*)

chapman NOUN a chapman was a trader or merchant ❑ *Not uttered by base sale of chapman's tongues* (*Love's Labours Lost 2.1*)

chaps, chops NOUN chaps (and chops) was a word for jaws ❑ *Which ne'er shook hands nor bade farewell to him/ Till he unseamed him from the nave to th' chops* (*Macbeth 1.2*)

chattels NOUN chattels were your moveable possessions. The word is used in the traditional marriage ceremony ❑ *She is my goods, my chattels* (*The Taming of the Shrew 3.3*)

chide VERB if you are chided by someone you are told off or reprimanded ❑ *Now I but chide, but I should use thee worse* (*A Midsummer Night's Dream 3.2*)

chinks NOUN chinks was a word for cash or money ❑ *he that can lay hold of her/ Shall have the chinks* (*Romeo and Juliet 1.5*)

choleric ADJ if something was called choleric it meant that they were quick to get angry ❑ *therewithal unruly waywardness that infirm and choleric years bring with them* (*King Lear 1.1*)

chuff NOUN a chuff was a miser,

someone who clings to his or her money ❏ *ye fat chuffs* (*Henry IV part I 2.2*)

cipher NOUN cipher here means nothing ❏ *Mine were the very cipher of a function* (*Measure for Measure 2.2*)

circummured ADJ circummured means that something is surrounded with a wall ❏ *He hath a garden circummured with brick* (*Measure for Measure 4.1*)

civet NOUN a civet is a type of scent or perfume ❏ *Give me an ounce of civet* (*King Lear 4.6*)

clamorous ADJ clamorous means noisy or boisterous ❏ *Be clamorous and leap all civil bounds* (*Twelfth Night 1.4*)

clangour, clangor NOUN clangour is a word that means ringing (the sound that bells make) ❏ *Like to a dismal clangour heard from far* (*Henry VI part III 2.3*)

cleave VERB if you cleave to something you stick to it or are faithful to it ❏ *Thy thoughts I cleave to* (*The Tempest 4.1*)

clock and clock, 'twixt PHRASE from hour to hour, without stopping or continuously ❏ *To weep 'twixt clock and clock* (*Cymbeline 3.4*)

close ADJ here close means hidden ❏ *Stand close; this is the same Athenian* (*A Midsummer Night's Dream 3.2*)

cloud NOUN a cloud on your face means that you have a troubled, unhappy expression ❏ *He has cloud in's face* (*Anthony and Cleopatra 3.2*)

cloy VERB if you cloy an appetite you satisfy it ❏ *Other women cloy/The*

appetites they feed (*Anthony and Cleopatra 2.2*)

cock-a-hoop, set PHRASE if you set cock-a-hoop you become free of everything ❏ *You will set cock-a-hoop* (*Romeo and Juliet 1.5*)

colours NOUN colours is a word used to describe battle-flags or banners. Sometimes we still say that we nail our colours to the mast if we are stating which team or side of an argument we support ❏ *the approbation of those that weep this lamentable divorce under her colours* (*Cymbeline 1.5*)

combustion NOUN combustion was a word meaning disorder or chaos ❏ *prophesying ... Of dire combustion and confused events* (*Macbeth 2.3*)

comely ADJ if you are or something is comely you or it is lovely, beautiful, graceful ❏ *O, what a world is this, when what is comely/Envenoms him that bears it!* (*As You Like It 2.3*)

commend VERB if you commend yourself to someone you send greetings to them ❏ *Commend me to my brother* (*Measure for Measure 1.4*)

compact NOUN a compact is an agreement or a contract ❏ *what compact mean you to have with us?* (*Julius Caesar 3.1*)

compass 1 NOUN here compass means range or scope ❏ *you would sound me from my lowest note to the top of my compass* (*Hamlet 3.2*) 2 VERB to compass here means to achieve, bring about or make happen ❏ *How now shall this be compassed?/Canst thou bring me to the party?* (*Tempest 3.2*)

comptible ADJ comptible is an old word meaning sensitive ❏ *I am very comptible, even to the least sinister usage.* (*Twelfth Night 1.5*)

confederacy NOUN a confederacy is a group of people usually joined together to commit a crime. It is another word for a conspiracy ❏ *Lo, she is one of this confederacy!* (*A Midsummer Night's Dream 3.2*)

confound VERB if you confound something you confuse it or mix it up; it also means to stop or prevent ❏ *A million fail, confounding oath on oath.* (*A Midsummer Night's Dream 3.2*)

contagion NOUN contagion is an old word for disease or poison ❏ *hell itself breathes out/ Contagion to this world* (*Hamlet 3.2*)

contumely NOUN contumely is an old word for an insult ❏ *the proud man's contumely* (*Hamlet 3.1*)

counterfeit 1 VERB if you counterfeit something you copy or imitate it ❏ *Meantime your cheeks do counterfeit our roses* (*Henry VI part I 2.4*) 2 VERB in this context counterfeit means to pretend or make believe ❏ *I will counterfeit the bewitchment of some popular man* (*Coriolanus*)

coz NOUN coz was a shortened form of the word cousin ❏ *sweet my coz, be merry* (*As You Like It 1.2*)

cozenage NOUN cozenage is an old word meaning cheating or a deception ❏ *Thrown out his angle for my proper life,/ And with such coz'nage* (*Hamlet 5.2*)

crave VERB crave used to mean to beg or request ❏ *I crave your pardon* (*The Comedy of Errors 1.2*)

crotchet NOUN crotchets are strange ideas or whims ❏ *thou hast some strange crotchets in thy head now* (*The Merry Wives of Windsor 2.1*)

cuckold NOUN a cuckold is a man whose wife has been unfaithful to him ❏ *As there is no true cuckold but calamity* (*Twelfth Night 1.5*)

cuffs, go to PHRASE this phrase meant to fight ❏ *the player went to cuffs in the question* (*Hamlet 2.2*)

cup VERB in this context cup is a verb which means to pour drink or fill glasses with alcohol ❏ *cup us til the world go round* (*Anthony and Cleopatra 2.7*)

cur NOUN cur is an insult meaning dog and is also used to mean coward ❏ *Out, dog! out, cur! Thou drivest me past the bounds/ Of maiden's patience* (*A Midsummer Night's Dream 3.2*)

curiously ADV in this context curiously means carefully or skilfully ❏ *The sleeves curiously cut* (*The Taming of the Shrew 4.3*)

curry VERB curry means to flatter or to praise someone more than they are worth ❏ *I would curry with Master Shallow that no man could better command his servants* (*Henry IV part II 5.1*)

custom NOUN custom is a habit or a usual practice ❏ *Hath not old custom made this life more sweet/ Than that of painted pomp?* (*As You Like It 2.1*)

cutpurse NOUN a cutpurse is an old word for a thief. Men used to carry their money in small bags (purse) that hung from their belts; thieves would cut the purse from the belt and steal their money ❏ *A cutpurse of the empire and the rule* (*Hamlet 3.4*)

dainty ADJ dainty used to mean splendid, fine ❏ *Why, that's my dainty Ariel!* (*Tempest 5.1*)

dally VERB if you dally with something you play with it or tease it ❏ *They that dally nicely with words may quickly make them wanton* (*Twelfth Night 3.1*)

damask COLOUR damask is a light-red or pink colour ❏ *Twas just the difference/Betwixt the constant red and mingled damask* (*As You Like It 3.5*)

dare 1 VERB dare means to challeng or, confront ❏ *He goes before me, and still dares me on* (*A Midsummer Night's Dream 3.3*) 2 VERB dare in this context means to present, deliver or inflict ❏ *all that fortune, death, and danger dare* (*Hamlet 4.4*)

darkly ADV darkly was used in this context to mean secretly or cunningly ❏ *I will go darkly to work with her* (*Measure for Measure 5.1*)

daw NOUN a daw was a slang term for idiot or fool (after the bird jackdaw which was famous for its stupidity) ❏ *Yea, just so much as you may take upon a knife's point and choke a daw withal* (*Much Ado About Nothing 3.1*)

debile ADJ debile meant weak or feeble ❏ *And debile minister great power* (*All's Well That Ends Well 2.3*)

deboshed ADJ deboshed was another way of saying corrupted or debauched ❏ *Men so disordered, deboshed and bold* (*King Lear 1.4*)

decoct VERB to decoct was to heat up, warm something ❏ *Can sodden water,/A drench for sur-reained jades*

... Decoct their cold blood to such valiant heat? (*Henry V 3.5*)

deep-revolving ADJ deep-revolving here uses the idea that you turn something over in your mind when you are thinking hard about it and so means deep-thinking, meditating ❏ *The deep-revolving Buckingham/No more shall be the neighbour to my counsels* (*Richard III 4.2*)

defect NOUN defect here means shortcoming or something that is not right ❏ *Being unprepared/Our will became the servant to defect* (*Macbeth 2.1*)

degree 1 NOUN degree here means rank, standing or station ❏ *Should a like language use to all degrees,/And mannerly distinguishment leave out/Betwixt the prince and beggar* (*The Winter's Tale 2.1*) 2 NOUN in this context, degree means extent or measure ❏ *her offence/Must be of such unnatural degree* (*King Lear 1.1*)

deify VERB if you deify something or someone you worship it or them as a God ❏ *all.. deifying the name of Rosalind* (*As You Like It 3.2*)

delated ADJ delated here means detailed ❏ *the scope/Of these delated articles* (*Hamlet 1.2*)

delicate ADJ if something was described as delicate it meant it was of fine quality or valuable ❏ *thou wast a spirit too delicate* (*The Tempest 1.2*)

demise VERB in this context demise means to transmit, give or convey ❏ *what state ... Canst thou demise to any child of mine?* (*Richard III 4.4*)

deplore VERB to deplore means to express with grief or sorrow ❏ *Never more/Will I my master's tears to you deplore* (*Twelfth Night 3.1*)

depose VERB if you depose someone you make them take an oath, or swear something to be true ❏ *Depose him in the justice of his cause* (*Richard II 1.3*)

depositary NOUN a depositary is a trustee ❏ *Made you ... my depositary* (*King Lear 2.4*)

derive 1 VERB to derive means to comes from or to descend (it usually applies to people) ❏ *No part of it is mine,/This shame derives itself from unknown loins.* (*Much Ado About Nothing 4.1*) 2 VERB if you derive something from someone you inherit it ❏ *Treason is not inherited ...Or, if we derive it from our friends/What's that to me?* (*As You Like It 1.3*)

descry VERB to see or catch sight of ❏ *The news is true, my lord. He is descried* (*Anthony and Cleopatra 3.7*)

desert 1 NOUN desert means worth or merit ❏ *That dost in vile misprison shackle up/My love and her desert* (*All's Well That Ends Well 2.3*) 2 ADJ desert is used here to mean lonely or isolated ❏ *if that love or gold/Can in this desert place buy entertainment* (*As You LIke It 2.4*)

design 1 VERB to design means to indicate or point out ❏ *we shall see/Justice design the victor's chivalry* (*Richard II 1.1*) 2 NOUN a design is a plan, an intention or an undertaking ❏ *hinder not the honour of his design* (*All's Well That Ends Well 3.6*)

designment NOUN a designment was a plan or undertaking ❏ *The*

desperate tempest hath so bang'd the Turks,/That their designment halts (*Othello 2.1*)

despite VERB despite here means to spite or attempt to thwart a plan ❏ *Only to despite them I will endeavour anything* (*Much Ado About Nothing 2.2*)

device NOUN a device is a plan, plot or trick ❏ *Excellent, I smell a device* (*Twelfth Night 2.3*)

disable VERB to disable here means to devalue or make little of ❏ *he disabled my judgement* (*As You Like It 5.4*)

discandy VERB here discandy means to melt away or dissolve ❏ *The hearts ... do discandy, melt their sweets* (*Anthony and Cleopatra 4.12*)

disciple VERB to disciple is to teach or train ❏ *He ...was/Discipled of the bravest* (*All's Well That Ends Well 1.2*)

discommend VERB if you discommend something you criticize it ❏ *my dialect which you discommend so much* (*King Lear 2.2*)

discourse NOUN discourse means conversation, talk or chat ❏ *which part of it I'll waste/With such discourse as I not doubt shall make it/Go quick away* (*The Tempest 5.1*)

discover VERB discover used to mean to reveal or show ❏ *the Prince discovered to Claudio that he loved my niece* (*Much Ado About Nothing 1.2*)

disliken VERB disguise, make unlike ❏ *disliken/The truth of your own seeming* (*The Winter's Tale 4.4*)

dismantle VERB to dismantle is to remove or take away ❏ *Commit a thing so monstrous to dismantle/*

So many folds of favour (*King Lear* 1.1)

disponge VERB disponge means to pour out or rain down ❏ *The poisonous damp of night disponge upon me* (*Anthony and Cleopatra* 4.9)

distrain VERB to distrain something is to confiscate it ❏ *My father's goods are all distrained and sold* (*Richard II* 2.3)

divers ADJ divers is an old word for various ❏ *I will give out divers schedules of my beauty* (*Twelfth Night* 1.5)

doff VERB to doff is to get rid of or dispose ❏ *make our women fight/ To doff their dire distresses* (*Macbeth* 4.3)

dog VERB if you dog someone or something you follow them or it closely ❏ *I will rather leave to see Hector than not to dog him* (*Troilus and Cressida* 5.1)

dotage NOUN dotage here means infatuation ❏ *Her dotage now I do begin to pity* (*A Midsummer Night's Dream* 4.1)

dotard NOUN a dotard was an old fool ❏ *I speak not like a dotard nor a fool* (*Much Ado About Nothing* 5.1)

dote VERB to dote is to love, cherish, care without seeing any fault ❏ *And won her soul; and she, sweet lady, dotes,/ Devoutly dotes, dotes in idolatry* (*A Midsummer Night's Dream* 1.1)

doublet NOUN a doublet was a man's close-fitting jacket with short skirt ❏ *Lord Hamlet, with his doublet all unbraced* (*Hamlet* 2.1)

dowager NOUN a dowager is a widow ❏ *Like to a step-dame or a dowage* (*A Midsummer Night's Dream* 1.1)

dowdy NOUN a dowdy was an ugly woman ❏ *Dido was a dowdy* (*Romeo and Juliet* 2.4)

dower NOUN a dower (or dowery) is the riches or property given by the father of a bride to her husband-to-be ❏ *Thy truth then by they dower* (*King Lear* 1.1)

dram NOUN a dram is a tiny amount ❏ *Why, everything adheres together that no dram of a scruple* (*Twelfth Night* 3.4)

drift NOUN drift is a plan, scheme or intention ❏ *Shall Romeo by my letters know our drift* (*Romeo and Juliet* 4.1)

dropsied ADJ dropsied means pretentious ❏ *Where great additions swell's and virtues none/ It is a dropsied honour* (*All's Well That Ends Well* 2.3)

drudge NOUN a drudge was a slave, servant ❏ *If I be his cuckold, he's my drudge* (*All's Well That Ends Well* 1.3)

dwell VERB to dwell sometimes meant to exist, to be ❏ *I'd rather dwell in my necessity* (*Merchant of Venice* 1.3)

earnest ADJ an earnest was a pledge to pay or a payment in advance ❏ *for an earnest of a greater honour/ He bade me from him call thee Thane of Cawdor* (*Macbeth* 1.3)

ecstasy NOUN madness ❏ *This is the very ecstasy of love* (*Hamlet* 2.1)

edict NOUN law or declaration ❏ *It stands as an edict in destiny.* (*A Midsummer Night's Dream* 1.1)

egall ADJ egall is an old word meaning equal ❏ *companions/Whose souls do bear an egall yoke of love* (Merchant of Venice 2.4)

eisel NOUN eisel meant vinegar ❏ *Woo't drink up eisel?* (Hamlet 5.1)

eke, eke out VERB eke meant to add to, to increase. Eke out nowadays means to make something last as long as possible – particularly in the sense of making money last a long time ❏ *Still be kind/And eke out our performance with your mind* (Henry V Chorus)

elbow, out at PHRASE out at elbow is an old phrase meaning in poor condition – as when your jacket sleeves are worn at the elbow which shows that it is an old jacket ❏ *He cannot, sir. He's out at elbow* (Measure for Measure 2.1)

element NOUN elements were thought to be the things from which all things were made. They were: air, earth, water and fire ❏ *Does not our lives consist of the four elements?* (Twelfth Night 2.3)

elf VERB to elf was to tangle ❏ *I'll ... elf all my hairs in knots* (King Lear 2.3)

embassy NOUN an embassy was a message ❏ *We'll once more hear Orsino's embassy.* (Twelfth Night 1.5)

emphasis NOUN emphasis here means a forceful expression or strong statement ❏ *What is he whose grief/Bears such an emphasis* (Hamlet 5.1)

empiric NOUN an empiric was an untrained doctor sometimes called a quack ❏ *we must not ... prostitute our past-cure malady/To empirics* (All's Well That Ends Well 2.1)

emulate ADJ emulate here means envious ❏ *pricked on by a most emulate pride* (Hamlet 1.1)

enchant VERB to enchant meant to put a magic spell on ❏ *Damn'd as thou art, thou hast enchanted her,/For I'll refer me to all things of sense* (Othello 1.2)

enclog VERB to enclog was to hinder something or to provide an obstacle to it ❏ *Traitors enscarped to enclog the guitless keel* (Othello 1.2)

endure VERB to endure was to allow or to permit ❏ *and will endure/Our setting down before't.* (Macbeth 5.4)

enfranchise VERB if you enfranchised something you set it free ❏ *Do this or this;/Take in that kingdom and enfranchise that;/Perform't, or else we damn thee.'* (Anthony and Cleopatra 1.1)

engage VERB to engage here means to pledge or to promise ❏ *This to be true I do engage my life* (As You Like It 5.4)

engaol VERB to lock up or put in prison ❏ *Within my mouth you have engaoled my tongue* (Richard II 1.3)

engine NOUN an engine was a plot, device or a machine ❏ *their promises, enticements, oaths, tokens, and all these engines, of lust, are not the things they go under* (All's Well That Ends Well 3.5)

englut VERB if you were engulfed you were swallowed up or eaten whole ❏ *For certainly thou art so near the gulf,/Thou needs must be englutted.* (Henry V 4.3)

enjoined ADJ enjoined describes people joined together for the same reason ❏ *Of enjoined penitents/*

There's four or five (All's Well That Ends Well 3.5)

entertain 1 VERB to entertain here means to welcome or receive ❑ *Approach, rich Ceres, her to entertain. (The Tempest 4.1)* 2 VERB to entertain in this context means to cherish, hold in high regard or to respect ❑ *and I quake,/ Lest thou a feverous life shouldst entertain/ And six or seven winters more respect/ Than a perpetual honour. (Measure for Measure 3.1)* 3 VERB to entertain means here to give something consideration ❑ *But entertain it,/ And though you think me poor, I am the man/ Will give thee all the world. (Anthony and Cleopatra 2.7)* 4 VERB to entertain here means to treat or handle ❑ *your highness is not entertained with that ceremonious affection as you were wont (King Lear 1.4)*

envious ADJ envious meant spiteful or vindictive ❑ *he shall appear to the envious a scholar (Measure for Measure 3.2)*

ere PREP ere was a common word for before ❑ *ere this I should ha' fatted all the region kites (Hamlet 2.2)*

err VERB to err means to go astray, to make a mistake ❑ *And as he errs, doting on Hermia's eyes (A Midsummer Night's Dream 1.1)*

erst ADV erst was a common word for once or before ❑ *that erst brought sweetly forth/ The freckled cowslip (Henry V 5.2)*

eschew VERB if you eschew something you deliberately avoid doing it ❑ *What cannot be eschewed must be embraced (The Merry Wives of Windsor 5.5)*

escote VERB to escote meant to pay for, support ❑ *How are they escoted? (Hamlet 2.2)*

estimable ADJ estimable meant appreciative ❑ *I could not with such estimable wonder over-far believe that (Twelfth Night 2.1)*

extenuate VERB extenuate means to lessen ❑ *Which by no means we may extenuate (A Midsummer Night's Dream 1.1)*

fain ADV fain was a common word meaning gladly or willingly ❑ *I would fain prove so (Hamlet 2.2)*

fall NOUN in a voice or music fall meant going higher and lower ❑ *and so die/ That strain again! it had a dying fall (Twelfth Night 1.1)*

false ADJ false was a common word for treacherous ❑ *this is counter, you false Danish dogs! (Hamlet 4.5)*

fare VERB fare means to get on or manage ❑ *I fare well (The Taming of the Shrew Introduction 2)*

feign VERB to feign was to make up, pretend or fake ❑ *It is the more like to be feigned (Twelfth Night 1.5)*

fie EXCLAM fie was an exclamation of disgust ❑ *Fie, that you'll say so! (Twelfth Night 1.3)*

figure VERB to figure was to symbolize or look like ❑ *Wings and no eyes, figure unheedy haste (A Midsummer Night's Dream 1.1)*

filch VERB if you filch something you steal it ❑ *With cunning hast thou filch'd my daughter's heart (A Midsummer Night's Dream 1.1)*

flout VERB to flout something meant to scorn it ❑ *Why will you suffer her to flout me thus? (A Midsummer Night's Dream 3.2)*

fond ADJ fond was a common word meaning foolish ❑ *Shall we their fond pageant see?* (*A Midsummer Night's Dream 3.2*)

footing 1 NOUN footing meant landing on shore, arrival, disembarkation ❑ *Whose footing here anticipates our thoughts/A se'nnight's speed.* (*Othello 2.1*) 2 NOUN footing also means support ❑ *there your charity would have lacked footing* (*Winter's Tale 3.3*)

forsooth ADV in truth, certainly, truly ❑ *I had rather, forsooth, go before you like a man* (*The Merry Wives of Windsor 3.2*)

forswear VERB if you forswear you lie, swear falsely or break your word ❑ *he swore a thing to me on Monday night, which he forswore on Tuesday morning* (*Much Ado About Nothing 5.1*)

freshes NOUN a fresh is a fresh water stream ❑ *He shall drink nought brine, for I'll not show him/Where the quick freshes are.* (*Tempest 3.2*)

furlong NOUN a furlong is a measure of distance. It is the equivalent on one eight of a mile ❑ *Now would I give a thousand furlongs of sea for an acre of barren ground* (*Tempest 1.1*)

gaberdine NOUN a gaberdine is a cloak ❑ *My best way is to creep under his gaberdine* (*Tempest 2.2*)

gage NOUN a gage was a challenge to duel or fight ❑ *There is my gage, Aumerle, in gage to thine* (*Richard II 4.1*)

gait NOUN your gait is your way of walking or step ❑ *I know her by her gait* (*Tempest 4.1*)

gall VERB to gall is to annoy or irritate ❑ *Let it not gall your patience, good Iago,/That I extend my manners* (*Othello 2.1*)

gambol NOUN frolic or play ❑ *Hop in his walks, and gambol in his eyes* (*A Midsummer Night's Dream 3.1*)

gaskins NOUN gaskins is an old word for trousers ❑ *or, if both break, your gaskins fall.* (*Twelfth Night 1.5*)

gentle ADJ gentle means noble or well-born ❑ *thrice-gentle Cassio!* (*Othello 3.4*)

glass NOUN a glass was another word for a mirror ❑ *no woman's face remember/Save from my glass, mine own* (*Tempest 3.1*)

gleek VERB to gleek means to make a joke or jibe ❑ *Nay, I can gleek upon occasion* (*A Midsummer Night's Dream 3.1*)

gust NOUN gust meant taste, desire or enjoyment. We still say that if you do something with gusto you do it with enjoyment or enthusiasm ❑ *the gust he hath in quarrelling* (*Twelfth Night 1.3*)

habit NOUN habit means clothes ❑ *You know me by my habit* (*Henry V 3.6*)

heaviness NOUN heaviness means sadness or grief ❑ *So sorrow's heaviness doth heavier grow/For debt that bankrupt sleep doth sorrow owe* (*A Midsummer Night's Dream 3.2*)

heavy ADJ if you are heavy you are said to be sad or sorrowful ❑ *Away from light steals home my heavy son* (*Romeo and Juliet 1.1*)

hie VERB to hie meant to hurry ❑ *My husband hies him home* (*All Well That Ends Well 4.4*)

hollowly ADV if you did something hollowly you did it insincerely ❑ *If hollowly invert/What best is boded me to mischief!* (*Tempest 3.1*)

holy-water, court PHRASE if you court holy water you make empty promises, or make statements which sound good but have no real meaning ❑ *court holy-water in a dry house is better than this rain-water out o'door* (*King Lear 3.2*)

howsoever ADV howsoever was often used instead of however ❑ *But howsoever strange and admirable* (*A Midsummer Night's Dream 5.1*)

humour NOUN your humour was your mood, frame of mind or temperament ❑ *it fits my humour well* (*As You Like It 3.2*)

ill ADJ ill means bad ❑ *I must thank him only,/Let my remembrance suffer ill report* (*Antony and Cleopatra 2.2*)

indistinct ADJ inseparable or unable to see a difference ❑ *Even till we make the main and the aerial blue/An indistinct regard.* (*Othello 2.1*)

indulgence NOUN indulgence meant approval ❑ *As you from crimes would pardoned be,/Let your indulgence set me free* (*The Tempest Epilogue*)

infirmity NOUN infirmity was weakness or fraility ❑ *Be not disturbed with my infirmity* (*The Tempest 4.1*)

intelligence NOUN here intelligence means information ❑ *Pursue her; and for this intelligence/If I have thanks* (*A Midsummer Night's Dream 1.1*)

inwards NOUN inwards meant someone's internal organs ❑ *the thought whereof/Doth like a poisonous mineral gnaw my inwards* (*Othello 2.1*)

issue 1 NOUN the issue of a marriage are the children ❑ *To thine and Albany's issues,/Be this perpetual* (*King Lear 1.1*) 2 NOUN in this context issue means outcome or result ❑ *I am to pray you, not to strain my speech,/To grosser issues* (*Othello*)

kind NOUN kind here means situation or case ❑ *But in this kind, wanting your father's voice,/The other must be held the worthier.* (*A Midsummer Night's Dream 1.1*)

knave NOUN a knave was a common word for scoundrel ❑ *How absolute the knave is!* (*Hamlet 5.1*)

league NOUN A distance. A league was the distance a person could walk in one hour ❑ *From Athens is her house remote seven leagues* (*A Midsummer Night's Dream 1.1*)

lief, had as ADJ I had as lief means I should like just as much ❑ *I had as lief the town crier spoke my lines* (*Hamlet 1.2*)

livery NOUN livery was a costume, outfit, uniform usually worn by a servant ❑ *You can endure the livery of a nun* (*A Midsummer Night's Dream 1.1*)

loam NOUN loam is soil containing decayed vegetable matter and therefore good for growing crops and plants ❑ *and let him have some plaster, or some loam, or some rough-cast about him, to signify wall* (*A Midsummer Night's Dream 3.1*)

lusty ADJ lusty meant strong ❑ *and oared/Himself with his good arms in lusty stroke/To th' shore* (*The Tempest 2.1*)

maidenhead NOUN maidenhead means chastity or virginity ❏ *What I am, and what I would, are as secret as maidenhead* (*Twelfth Night 1.5*)

mark VERB mark means to note or pay attention to ❏ *Where sighs and groans,/ Are made not marked* (*Macbeth 4.3*)

marvellous ADJ very or extremely ❏ *here's a marvellous convenient place for our rehearsal* (*A Midsummer Night's Dream 3.1*)

meet ADJ right or proper ❏ *tis most meet you should* (*Macbeth 5.1*)

merely ADV completely or entirely ❏ *Love is merely a madness* (*As You Like It 3.2*)

misgraffed ADJ misgraffed is an old word for mismatched or unequal ❏ *Or else misgraffed in respect of years* (*A Midsummer Night's Dream 1.1*)

misprision NOUN a misprision meant an error or mistake ❏ *Misprision in the highest degree!* (*Twelfth Night 1.5*)

mollification NOUN mollification is appeasement or a way of preventing someone getting angry ❏ *I am to hull here a little longer. Some mollification for your giant* (*Twelfth Night 1.5*)

mouth, cold in the PHRASE a well-known saying of the time which meant to be dead ❏ *What, must our mouths be cold?* (*The Tempest 1.1*)

murmur NOUN murmur was another word for rumour or hearsay ❏ *and then 'twas fresh in murmur* (*Twelfth Night 1.2*)

murrain NOUN murrain was another word for plague, pestilence ❏ *A murrain on your monster, and* the devil take your fingers!* (*The Tempest 3.2*)

neaf NOUN neaf meant fist ❏ *Give me your neaf, Monsieur Mustardseed* (*A Midsummer Night's Dream 4.1*)

nice 1 ADJ nice had a number of meanings here it means fussy or particular ❏ *An therefore, goaded with most sharp occasions,/ Which lay nice manners by, I put you to/ The use of your own virtues* (*All's Well That Ends Well 5.1*) 2 ADJ nice here means critical or delicate ❏ *We're good... To set so rich a man/ On the nice hazard of one doubtful hour?* (*Henry IV part 1*) 3 ADJ nice in this context means carefully accurate, fastidious ❏ *O relation/ Too nice and yet too true!* (*Macbeth 4.3*) 4 ADJ trivial, unimportant ❏ *Romeo .. Bid him bethink/ How nice the quarrel was* (*Romeo and Juliet 3.1*)

nonpareil NOUN if you are nonpareil you are without equal, peerless ❏ *though you were crown'd/ The nonpareil of beauty!* (*Twelfth Night 1.5*)

office NOUN office here means business or work ❏ *Speak your office* (*Twelfth Night 1.5*)

outsport VERB outsport meant to overdo ❏ *Let's teach ourselves that honorable stop,/ Not to outsport discretion.* (*Othello 2.2*)

owe VERB owe meant own, possess ❏ *Lend less than thou owest* (*King Lear 1.4*)

paragon 1 VERB to paragon was to surpass or excede ❏ *he hath achieved a maid/ That paragons description and wild fame* (*Othello 2.1*) 2 VERB to paragon could also mean to compare with ❏ *I will give thee*

bloody teeth If thou with Caesar
paragon again/ My man of men
(Anthony and Cleopatra 1.5)

pate NOUN pate is another word for
head ❏ Back, slave, or I will break
thy pate across (The Comedy of
Errors 2.1)

paunch VERB to paunch someone
is to stab (usually in the stomach).
Paunch is still a common word for a
stomach ❏ Batter his skull, or
paunch him with a stake (The
Tempest 3.2)

peevish ADJ if you are peevish you
are irritable or easily angered ❏ Run
after that same peevish messenger
(Twelfth Night 1.5)

peradventure ADV perhaps or
maybe ❏ Peradventure this is not
Fortune's work (As You Like It 1.2)

perforce 1 ADV by force or violently
❏ my rights and royalties,/ Plucked
from my arms perforce (Richard
II 2.3) 2 ADV necessarily ❏ The
hearts of men, they must perforce have
melted (Richard II 5.2)

personage NOUN personage
meant your appearance ❏ Of what
personage and years is he? (Twelfth
Night 1.5)

pestilence NOUN pestilence was a
common word for plague or disease
❏ Methought she purg'd the air of
pestilence! (Twelfth Night 1.1)

physic NOUN physic was medicine
or a treatment ❏ tis a physic/ That's
bitter to sweet end (Measure for
Measure 4.6)

place NOUN place means a person's
position or rank ❏ Sons, kinsmen,
thanes,/ And you whose places are the
nearest (Macbeth 1.4)

post NOUN here a post means a
messenger ❏ there are twenty weak
and wearied posts/ Come from the
north (Henry IV part II 2.4)

pox NOUN pox was a word for any
disease during which the victim
had blisters on the skin. It was
also a curse, a swear word ❏ The
pox of such antic, lisping, affecting
phantasims (Romeo and Juliet 2.4)

prate VERB to prate means to chatter
❏ if thou prate of mountains
(Hamlet 5.1)

prattle VERB to prattle is to chatter
or talk without purpose ❏ I prattle
out of fashion, and I dote In mine own
comforts (Othello 2.1)

precept NOUN a precept was an
order or command ❏ and my father's
precepts I therein do forget. (The
Tempest 3.1)

present ADJ present here means
immediate ❏ We'll put the matter to
the present push (Hamlet 5.1)

prithee EXCLAM prithee is the
equivalent of please or may I ask
– a polite request ❏ I prithee, and
I'll pay thee bounteously (Twelfth
Night 1.2)

prodigal NOUN a prodigal is
someone who wastes or squanders
money ❏ he's a very fool, and a
prodigal (Twelfth Night 1.3)

purpose NOUN purpose is used here
to mean intention ❏ understand my
purposes aright (King Lear 1.4)

quaff VERB quaff was a common
word which meant to drink heavily
or take a big drink ❏ That quaffing
and drinking will undo you (Twelfth
Night 1.3)

quaint 1 ADJ clever, ingenious ❑ *with a quaint device* (*The Tempest 3.3*) 2 ADJ cunning ❑ *I'll... tell quaint lies* (*Merchant of Venice 3.4*) 3 ADJ pretty, attractive ❑ *The clamorous owl, that nightly hoots and wonders/At our quaint spirit* (*A Midsummer Night's Dream 2.2*)

quoth VERB an old word which means say ❑ *Tis dinner time.' quoth I* (*The Comedy of Errors 2.1*)

rack NOUN a rack described clouds or a cloud formation ❑ *And, like this insubstantial pageant faded,/ Leave not a rack behind* (*The Tempest 4.1*)

rail VERB to rant or swear at. It is still used occasionally today ❑ *Why do I rail on thee* (*Richard II 5.5*)

rate NOUN rate meant estimate, opinion ❑ *My son is lost, and, in my rate, she too* (*The Tempest 2.1*)

recreant NOUN recreant is an old word which means coward ❑ *Come, recreant, come, thou child* (*A Midsummer Night's Dream 3.2*)

remembrance NOUN remembrance is used here to mean memory or recollection ❑ *our remembrances of days foregone* (*All's Well That Ends Well 1.3*)

resolute ADJ firm or not going to change your mind ❑ *You are resolute, then?* (*Twelfth Night 1.5*)

revels NOUN revels means celebrations or a party ❑ *Our revels now are ended* (*The Tempest 4.1*)

rough-cast NOUN a mixture of lime and gravel (sometimes shells too) for use on an outer wall ❑ *and let him have some plaster, or some loam, or some rough-cast about him, to signify wall* (*A Midsummer Night's Dream 3.1*)

sack NOUN sack was another word for wine ❑ *My man-monster hath drowned his tongue in sack.* (*The Tempest 3.2*)

sad ADJ in this context sad means serious, grave ❑ *comes me the Prince and Claudio... in sad conference* (*Much Ado About Nothing 1.3*)

sampler NOUN a piece of embroidery, which often showed the family tree ❑ *Both on one sampler, sitting on one cushion* (*A Midsummer Night's Dream 3.2*)

saucy ADJ saucy means rude ❑ *I heard you were saucy at my gates* (*Twelfth Night 1.5*)

schooling NOUN schooling means advice ❑ *I have some private schooling for you both.* (*A Midsummer Night's Dream 1.1*)

seething ADJ seething in this case means boiling – we now use seething when we are very angry ❑ *Lovers and madmen have such seething brains* (*A Midsummer Night's Dream 5.1*)

semblative ADJ semblative means resembling or looking like ❑ *And all is semblative a woman's part.* (*Twelfth Night 1.4*)

several ADJ several here means separate or different ❑ *twenty several messengers* (*Anthony and Cleopatra 1.5*)

shrew NOUN An annoying person or someone who makes you cross ❑ *Bless you, fair shrew.* (*Twelfth Night 1.3*)

AS YOU LIKE IT

shroud VERB to shroud is to hide or shelter ❏ *I will here, shroud till the dregs of the storm be past* (*The Tempest 2.2*)

sickleman NOUN a sickleman was someone who used a sickle to harvest crops ❏ *You sunburnt sicklemen, of August weary* (*The Tempest 4.1*)

soft ADV soft here means wait a moment or stop ❏ *But, soft, what nymphs are these* (*A Midsummer Night's Dream 4.1*)

something ADV something here means somewhat or rather ❏ *Be something scanter of your maiden presence* (*Hamlet 1.3*)

sooth NOUN truly ❏ *Yes, sooth; and so do you* (*A Midsummer Night's Dream 3.2*)

spleen NOUN spleen means fury or anger ❏ *That, in a spleen, unfolds both heaven and earth* (*A Midsummer Night's Dream 1.1*)

sport NOUN sport means recreation or entertainment ❏ *I see our wars/ Will turn unto a peaceful comic sport* (*Henry VI part I 2.2*)

strain NOUN a strain is a tune or a musical phrase ❏ *and so die/ That strain again! it had a dying fall* (*Twelfth Night 1.1*)

suffer VERB in this context suffer means perish or die ❏ *but an islander that hath lately suffered by a thunderbolt.* (*The Tempest 2.2*)

suit NOUN a suit is a petition, request or proposal (marriage) ❏ *Because she will admit no kind of suit* (*Twelfth Night 1.2*)

sup VERB to sup is to have supper ❏ *Go know of Cassio where he supped tonight* (*Othello 5.1*)

surfeit NOUN a surfeit is an amount which is too large ❏ *If music be the food of love, play on;/ Give me excess of it, that, surfeiting,/ The appetite may sicken* (*Twelfth Night 1.1*)

swain NOUN a swain is a suitor or person who wants to marry ❏ *take this transformed scalp/ From off the head of this Athenian swain* (*A Midsummer Night's Dream 4.1*)

thereto ADV thereto meant also ❏ *If she be black, and thereto have a wit* (*Othello 2.1*)

throstle NOUN a throstle was a name for a song-bird ❏ *The throstle with his note so true* (*A Midsummer Night's Dream 3.1*)

tidings NOUN tidings meant news ❏ *that upon certain tidings now arrived, importing the mere perdition of the Turkish fleet* (*Othello 2.2*)

transgress VERB if you transgress you break a moral law or rule of behaviour ❏ *Virtue that transgresses is but patched with sin* (*Twelfth Night 1.5*)

troth, by my PHRASE this phrase means I swear or in truth or on my word ❏ *By my troth, Sir Toby, you must come in earlier o' nights* (*Twelfth Night 1.3*)

trumpery NOUN trumpery means things that look expensive but are worth nothing (often clothing) ❏ *The trumpery in my house, go bring it hither/ For stale catch these thieves* (*The Tempest 4.1*)

twink NOUN In the wink of an eye or no time at all ❏ *Ay, with a twink* (*The Tempest 4.1*)

undone ADJ if something or someone is undone they are ruined, destroyed, brought down ❑ *You have undone a man of fourscore three* (*The Winter's Tale 4.4*)

varlets NOUN varlets were villains or ruffians ❑ *Say again: where didst thou leave these varlets?* (*The Tempest 4.1*)

vaward NOUN the vaward is an old word for the vanguard, front part or earliest ❑ *And since we have the vaward of the day* (*A Midsummer Night's Dream 4.1*)

visage NOUN face ❑ *when Phoebe doth behold/Her silver visage in the watery glass* (*A Midsummer Night's Dream 1.1*)

voice NOUN voice means vote ❑ *He has our voices* (*Coriolanus 2.3*)

waggish ADJ waggish means playful ❑ *As waggish boys in game themselves forswear* (*A Midsummer Night's Dream 1.1*)

wane VERB to wane is to vanish, go down or get slighter. It is most often used to describe a phase of the moon ❑ *but, O, methinks, how slow/This old moon wanes* (*A Midsummer Night's Dream 1.1*)

want VERB to want means to lack or to be without ❑ *a beast that wants discourse of reason/Would have mourned longer* (*Hamlet 1.2*)

warrant VERB to assure, promise, guarantee ❑ *I warrant your grace* (*As You Like It 1.2*)

welkin NOUN welkin is an old word for the sky or the heavens ❑ *The starry welkin cover thou anon/With drooping fog as black as Acheron* (*A Midsummer Night's Dream 3.2*)

wench NOUN wench is an old word for a girl ❑ *Well demanded, wench* (*The Tempest 1.2*)

whence ADV from where ❑ *Whence came you, sir?* (*Twelfth Night 1.5*)

wherefore ADV why ❑ *Wherefore, sweetheart? what's your metaphor?* (*Twelfth Night 1.3*)

wide-chopped ADJ if you were wide-chopped you were big-mouthed ❑ *This wide-chopped rascal* (*The Tempest 1.1*)

wight NOUN wight is an old word for person or human being ❑ *She was a wight, if ever such wight were* (*Othello 2.1*)

wit NOUN wit means intelligence or wisdom ❑ *thou didst conclude hairy men plain dealers, without wit* (*The Comedy of Errors 2.2*)

wits NOUN wits mean mental sharpness ❑ *we that have good wits have much to answer for* (*As You Like It 4.1*)

wont ADJ to wont is to be in the habit of doing something regularly ❑ *When were you wont to use my sister thus?* (*The Comedy of Errors 2.2*)

wooer NOUN a wooer is a suitor, someone who is hoping to marry ❑ *and of a foolish knight that you brought in one night here to be her wooer* (*Twelfth Night 1.3*)

wot VERB wot is an old word which means know or learn ❑ *for well I wot/Thou runnest before me* (*A Midsummer Night's Dream 3.2*)